angels

simply ®

angels

BELETA GREENAWAY

STERLING/ZAMBEZI
An imprint of Sterling Publishing Co., Inc.

New York / London
www.sterlingpublishing.com

dedication

I would like to dedicate this book to a very dear friend of mine called Catherine Coverdale. Without her help I would have found this book difficult to write, but her wisdom and encouragement gave me the confidence to continue.

Blessed be, Catherine!

STERLING and the distinctive Sterling logo are registered trademarks of Sterling Publishing Co., Inc.

Library of Congress Cataloging-in-Publication Data Available

2 4 6 8 10 9 7 5 3 1

Published by Sterling Publishing Co., Inc.
387 Park Avenue South, New York, NY 10016
Copyright © 2009 by Beleta Greenaway
Chapter opening illustrations © 2009 by Hannah Firmin
All other illustrations © 2009 by Tina Fong
Published in the UK solely by Zambezi Publishing Ltd
P.O. Box 221, Plymouth, Devon, PL2 2YJ UK
Distributed in Canada by Sterling Publishing
C/o Canadian Manda Group, 165 Dufferin Street
Toronto, Ontario, Canada M6K 3H6
Distributed in Australia by Capricorn Link (Australia) Pty. Ltd.
P.O. Box 704, Windsor, NSW 2756, Australia

Printed in China
All rights reserved

Sterling ISBN 978-1-4027-4493-8
Zambezi ISBN 978-1-903065-59-4

For information about custom editions, special sales, premium and corporate purchases, please contact Sterling Special Sales Department at 800-805-5489 or specialsales@sterlingpublishing.com.

contents

introduction

Wise men have said that the angels of the Creator departed this Earth after the fall of Atlantis, and because of that, human and angelic connection disappeared for many centuries. Other religions and faiths sprang up to take the angels' place, and then humans suddenly realized how much they missed the presence of angels and longed once more for their wisdom and loving guidance. Many of us now sense that angels have returned en masse to teach us and guide us to a higher consciousness. I feel that our acceptance of them dictates that we will soon have the ability to communicate much better with them. It does not matter what faith or religion you ascribe to; it is of little consequence to angels. All they want is for humans to get back to the "garden" and to the care of God.

Numerous books have been written about these wonderful beings, and I feel so privileged to be able to add my contribution. However, if you feel in your heart that you do not gravitate toward certain chapters in this book, or that the things that I say in this book don't connect with your truth, then you must trust your own intuition. It is a fact that we all go at our own paces and that we must all find our own ways forward.

For three decades I have worked as a clairvoyant, so some of you might wonder why, of all people, I am writing a book about angels, especially as some religious factions believe that to do the work I do, I must have sold my soul to the devil. Some believe this must be the case for me to be able to see into the future as I do, but the truth is that we all have the ability to know more than we think we do about the unseen world, as long as we decide to travel on that particular pathway. The clairvoyants whom I have met have been special souls who have helped so many. They are what we would call modern-day soothsayers, or spiritual life coaches, who through their readings can give focus to others in times of hardship and doubt. Sadly for many people, conventional religion does not seem to give them any spiritual hope. In my life, I have met many people who love my work and some who look down on me and all that I stand for. It doesn't bother me anymore because I have learned to take life as it comes and I understand that we cannot please all the people all the time.

BIGOTRY

On one occasion, I attended a very special wedding; at the reception I was seated with ten other people at a round table adorned with damask tablecloths and fine crystal. The middle-aged minister who had just conducted the wedding looked pointedly at me and asked what I did for a living. Suddenly there was silence as all eyes turned in my direction. Oh, dear, I thought. This is going to be difficult.

"I'm a clairvoyant," I said. He looked ruffled, and his little birdlike wife, who was sitting next to him, shifted uncomfortably in her seat.

"Umm," he replied pompously. "Are you aware of the seriousness of what you have just said?"

Slowly I put my knife and fork down on the plate and gave him my full attention. "I am sorry, but I don't quite understand you."

"You do realize that you could be denied entrance to Heaven when you pass over."

My mother had taught me never to argue about politics or religion, but here I was about to go into a full-scale debate. The preacher fixed me with a steely gaze and puffed up his chest in a self-important manner. "I'll pray for your soul, my child."

I got angry. We were here solely to celebrate the wedding of my dearest friend, and I knew this so-called man of God was champing at the bit and couldn't wait to force his opinions on me and the rest of the guests at our table. This was not why I had come to this happy event, and I felt resentful at being targeted. The others sucked in their breath, all eyes riveted on the tension between us. One of the guests leaned across and touched my arm sympathetically. With grim determination, I felt I had to ignore my mother's good advice and stick up for myself as I answered him quietly.

"I do believe in a divine being. I feel especially guided by angels, and I believe they are there in the afterlife. I also believe you are judged on your actions in life and not the particular church that you ascribe to. Being a clairvoyant is no sin. I am not a dreadful person, and my gift was given to me by God!"

Suddenly one of the other guests spoke up and agreed with me, and then another. One lady was an aromatherapist; another was a healer; and then a spiritualist joined the debate. The preacher was outnumbered, and he looked decidedly uncomfortable. This must have been the first time in his life that he had been unable to hide behind the authority of his position, and he mumbled under his breath that he was obviously the odd one out. Through this experience, I have realized that many of us have moved on and that many of us now have a more tolerant attitude toward other faiths and viewpoints.

The belief in angels is widespread in many cultures and religions, so I thought I would share with you some of my experiences encountering angels in my life. To some, they might seem small and insignificant, but in my heart I know the help and information I received was real. The skeptical would perhaps want more proof, but the angelic realms work in a very subtle way. I have read of fortunate people who have had mind-blowing encounters with angels, and at times I have really envied them and longed for the same experiences.

Mostly my encounters with angels have been intangible. "Was it my imagination? Did I really dream that? Did I hear that?" I no longer beat myself up about the whys and wherefores. I trust that any information the angels want to give me will be correct and that it will come at the right time. I say to my readers, if you fervently ask for help and information, you will receive it. If you feel unwell or depressed, ask the angels to rectify this, and you will see an improvement. Once the angels start to work with you, there will come a time when you get to "know" or "feel" them around you. It is just a matter of experimenting. I know they can create miracles and bring great peace of mind and strength to the suffering and the weak. Never think you are too small or insignificant for them to attend you. They love to be of service in any way they can. Now let us look at some true stories about angels.

1

ENCOUNTERS WITH ANGELS

ROBERT

In the middle of the 1950s, when I was about eleven years old, my sandy-haired stepbrother, Robert, was then just a toddler. Robert became seriously ill, and I can remember clearly one of his little ears being bright red and sticking out like a trumpet. The doctor was called immediately. Within a few hours, Robert was rushed to Frenchay Hospital in Bristol, England, with a critical brain tumor. Surgery was scheduled for the next day, but the surgeons gave him only a 10 percent chance of recovery. My mother, a simple country girl who came from a large family, was inconsolable.

At sunrise the following morning, she was lying in bed after a restless night's sleep. On the quilt a few feet away from her, a small image began to appear. It was a beautiful angel, about ten inches high, gently rocking a baby's crib, which had an iridescent glow over it. Staring straight at my mother, the angel wrapped her wings around the crib in a protective gesture, her gaze never leaving my mother's face. Gradually, after four or five minutes, the apparition faded, leaving my mother soothed and reassured. After a long illness, Robert did recover, and from that day forward my mother fervently believed in angels.

I often have dreams that come true, and I pay great attention to them, especially the dreams that occur between five and seven o'clock in the morning. This seems to be a time when our angels and spiritual guides like to converse with us, perhaps because we are just coming out of sleep and are in the right state of consciousness. It is a well-known fact that Wiccan white witches keep dream diaries, which they call the Book of Shadows. In this book they record their dreams and premonitions, dating them carefully. I have found with dream information that your informers usually give you a dream whose events will occur in a few days' time, but in the same dream, there could be an event that might happen two or three years in the future. This is why it is so important to write these dreams down and date them as soon as you can, and to note down as much detail as you can remember. One particular morning, I had a vivid and disturbing dream.

AN ANGEL OF DEATH

In the dream, my spiritual guide appeared and took me into a special room where I waited quite nervously for someone very important to come; even my guide seemed to be on edge.

Suddenly I became aware of a very tall and overpowering being staring right through me. He was dressed in a black frock coat with a snowy white cravat at his throat. His gaze was unrelenting as he locked minds with me. I was struck by how beautiful he was. He had thick dark hair, a long thin face, and liquid brown eyes, and his arms were folded firmly over his chest. I knew instinctively that he was one of the angels of death, and my next alarmed thought was, Well, this is it, Beleta; it looks like you are going to die, girl, and he's here to take you home.

His eyes held great compassion and deep love, telling me not to worry, as it was someone else who was going to pass over soon. I heard his thoughts in my head as he asked me to help him with an important project concerning this person in the near future. He said I would need to be in contact with many people, and he asked if I would mind doing this for him. I shook my head in complete awe and wondered why he had come to ask me, of all people, when there were far better folk for the job out there in the world than little ol' me!

And then he smiled and I was completely dazzled. He informed me that if it had been my time to go back into the spirit realm, his arms would have been wide open to welcome me. We both giggled a bit, and I marveled at the discovery that angels have a great sense of humor—even an angel of death!

I awoke with a start. Lying there, I wondered whether I had really been communicating with an angel of death, or whether my mother was right when she often remarked when I was a little girl, "Child, you've really got far too much imagination." If the dream was correct, then what exactly did the angel want me to do, and worse still, who was going to die?

Note:
Through extensive reading and angelic research, I had believed Metatron to be the primary angel of death, but this dream told me otherwise. There were numerous angels who were in service for this particular task. Many, for instance, would be needed when there were world disasters or war.

A few days later my doorbell rang, and two of my clients, Alan and Shirley, who were husband and wife, asked if they could come in as they had some important news. I ushered them into my living room, and they immediately told me they had been to see one of my friends, Irena, who was a well-known and well-loved spiritual healer in the area. Their appointment with her had been scheduled for ten o'clock that morning, but they could not understand why she had not answered the doorbell. A next-door neighbor came out and told them that Irena had had a brain hemorrhage while driving her car the previous evening, and that she had died.

After my clients had gone, I sat in total shock. Irena had no close family in the area. Her son was away, and no one knew that she had died! As Irena and I moved in the same social circles, I sat by my phone and had the dreadful task of informing everyone (even her ex-husband, whom she had recently divorced) of the sad news. After many telephone calls, I felt exhausted with the grief and tears of her friends and clients, to whom I was passing this sad news. Then I remembered the angel telling me that I would have to contact many people for him. This sad atmosphere prevailed for some weeks afterward because Irena's clients, who understandably couldn't locate her, contacted me to find out where she was.

When it came to the funeral, the crematorium was full, and I realized how this wonderful person had touched the lives of so many others and how she had given help and love to each and every one of them. It was only then that I knew how special she was to the spirit world too, especially the angel who had come to tell me of her death.

Note:
Through this experience I know that every little kindness we give to others is noted. From these acts of
kindness we gain unconditional love and thanks from
the angelic realms. I have also become aware of the
prior knowledge that these beings have of our
deaths, and the deaths of every creature. It would
seem that we can't hide anything from them.

DREAM WORK

Angels will cheer you up if you are at your wits' end; they
will connect with you, especially in dreams; and they will
encourage you toward dream work. Our days are far too
busy for us to find time for total peace and relaxation. Noise
pollution is a major factor in stopping us from connecting to
the Divine Source. Our ancestors did not have this problem
so much, as life was much simpler then. Most of us live in a
busy society, and we are often ruled by the clock, so sometimes we forget to reconnect with our spiritual center.

Only in sleep can we be our true selves and cast off the bur-
dens of everyday life. Many people claim that they never
dream or that they cannot remember their dreams, but we
all dream, and everything we dream about is embedded
deeply in our subconscious. Our brains are like sophisticated
computers, and we have to find the magic key to unlock all
the information that dwells within.

I remember as a child going to bed early so that I could connect with these wonderful beings and be reassured that
everything was okay. I loved art, and sometimes a creative
angel would show me interesting color blends and patterns

while I slept. I have always kept a dream diary, and have been amazed at how accurate some dreams are. If you want to connect with the angelic vibration or your spirit guide while you sleep, say a prayer for guidance and premonition in dream sleep. It is not rocket science, but be patient, as it may take a little time before you get it right. There will be times when you will be successful and others when nothing much happens. I am not sure whether angels have times when they will not link with us or whether these times are a result of our own inability to reach them.

ISLANDS IN THE SKY

One very vivid dream I had a few years ago has always stayed with me. Again I was taken to the spirit world and was asked by my spiritual guide to look up into the sky. There, high above us, was the most beautiful island in verdant shades of green, cream, and orange. Waterfalls tumbled down, and rainbows enveloped the whole island. From this dream I was taught about the beauty of the spirit world and how unlike our planet it is. Angels tend to this spirit realm, and they are constantly inventing new things to delight us when we return home.

Note:
Last year I was browsing a fantasy art sight on the Internet, and one of the artists had painted a beautiful island in the sky. Perhaps he had also been shown the vision of islands in the sky by his angel in dream sleep.

2

ANGELS IN THE MODERN WORLD

ANGEL CARDS

Today you can find many beautifully illustrated decks of angel cards in retail stores and on the Internet. They usually consist of forty to fifty cards depicting a colorful illustration of an angel and a short, uplifting saying on each one. I use cards like these at the end of my readings for clients who are spiritual and who love angels. You can also shuffle and pick one card for help and instruction in your day ahead, and usually the card you choose is very accurate. The cards can also be used in altar work. Select an angel card for the problem at hand. Place the card on the altar, alongside crystals, flowers, and other objects that are important to you; this will give the prayer much more atmosphere and devotion. If you want to connect with a particular angel in dream work, you can place one of the cards under your pillow at night, or you might prefer to use one in your meditation.

ANGEL WEB SITES

There are numerous Web sites that are dedicated to angels, and a wealth of information is out there for those who care to look. The Web sites connected to angel art are wonderful and all unique. When I have time, I like to look at the pictures. Today's artist seems to have a good understanding of the angel frequency and angels' esoteric grace. Some of the old-style painters from centuries past did not exactly do these wonderful beings justice, and some of them are in fact downright ugly! I find this particularly so with some of the paintings of cherubs.

Angels of the Zodiac

Some of the most important angels can also be linked to the signs of the Zodiac:

Aries:	Machidiel
Taurus:	Asmodel
Gemini:	Ambriel
Cancer:	Muriel
Leo:	Verchiel
Virgo:	Hamaliel
Libra:	Uriel
Scorpio:	Barbiel
Sagittarius:	Adnachie
Capricorn:	Hanael
Aquarius:	Gabriel
Pisces:	Barchiel

THE ANGEL OF THE NORTH

A gargantuan structure of an angel is located in the north of England at the head of the Team Valley, near Gateshead. It took five months to construct and was completed in February 1998. It is the largest angel construction known in the world today. The renowned artist Anthony Gormley created this imposing sculpture, and many of his other creations can be seen in Australia, the United States, Japan, Norway, and Ireland.

The grassy hilltop that the angel sculpture stands upon represents a megalithic mound. Beginning in the 1720s, the ground beneath was mined for coal for two hundred years. Anthony Gormley remarked that his creation of the angel in the light was a celebration of the hard work and industry of the men of the north who toiled beneath the surface in the darkness for so many years. The site was carefully chosen for maximum impact. The angel stands 65 feet (20 meters) high, about the same as a five-story building, and the wingspan is 175 feet (54 meters) wide, nearly the same width as the wingspan of a large Boeing airplane. Each wing reportedly weighs 50 tons

and the body perhaps 100 tons. The whole construction is of Cor-ten steel and has been made to last for a hundred years. It can withstand squalls and gales of up to 100 miles an hour, and on its shoulder blade is a door for internal access and inspection into the hollow body.

More than ninety thousand people a day drive by this angel, that is, about 33 million people a year. They marvel at its austerity and grandeur. Mysteriously, it has no features on its face. Many have said that as the light and weather change, so the expression on the angel's face changes, so this is truly a living sculpture. The artist remarked that he wanted to create a feeling of alertness and space from his creation, as a focus for our hopes and fears. The angel is catalytic for gatherings on New Year's Eve, pre-wedding ceremonies, and eclipses. It seems that this congregational site represents a link between the sky and the Earth, to connect us with the unknown and the known, and to remind us of our own mortality.

Note:
Many, especially in the media, have criticized the sculpture as being stark and ugly and the vast amount of money spent on it as wasteful, especially as the bulk of the funding came from the English National Lottery. Others love its simplicity and think it beautiful. I believe in this secular era that it has been brought into being to remind us that angels are here to stay, and perhaps because of it, a new consciousness will come into the world.

Some of my clients who have been fortunate enough to see a real angel have often remarked how large they are, often thirty to fifty feet high. So it does not surprise me that Anthony Gormley has chosen to represent his steel angel in this way.

3

ANGELS AND THE
SPIRITUAL WORLD

ANGEL MUSIC

One particular night, before I went to bed, I felt very low. For the past six weeks, most of my clients had been either suicidal or grieving for a dead child or spouse. I felt the weight of the world on my shoulders and I had had more than enough. Soon, I promised myself, I would start to look for another job doing something more cheerful and less responsible. I might even be able to lose some of the extra pounds of fat that had accumulated over the years due to sitting down to work all day long and listening to other people's problems.

"My work is one long dirge," I moaned as I pulled the duvet over my head and eventually fell into a grumpy sleep. As I am a very light sleeper, I remember most of what I dream. Right away, as I drifted off, I felt my guide approach me.

"And what is this mood about? Why are you sulking like a baby?" he said in a very matter-of-fact way.

"Life is full of doom and gloom; other people don't have to put up with all of this trouble," I said resentfully.

"But you chose this pathway before you reincarnated. You know you are in service!"

"Well, I must have been stark raving bonkers, and I don't care a bit what you think; I am going to get another job!"

He laughed good-naturedly and shook his head. "Oh, dear!

You are very willful, Beleta, but now, come on; get out of this bad mood. I have something I want you to see."

Seconds later, we were on the periphery of a spiritual realm that was truly beautiful. I knew from my guide not to move, as parts of it were out of bounds to living humans. I could feel an invisible force field separating me from this angelic world. From out of nowhere, the most haunting and ethereal music drifted over to us, and I can honestly say that I have never heard anything like it before or since. It seemed to be the music of all creation and all living things. As the notes reverberated, colors appeared in the atmosphere above us. They were the most amazing hues and were definitely not of our world! I stood transfixed as I listened to the angelic choir, and I felt their wings oscillating in rhythm to the melodies. Music on the earthly plane is nothing to this; it would not even stand in comparison. How I wished I had a tape recorder with me! Each note resonated to everything that was good within me. It reminded me of who we really are: of our sole purpose in the divine plan and the universal love, which is around all of us. I wanted to stay there forever, but I knew we had to leave. It was just a brief glimpse of a stunning angelic realm, and it was truly amazing. I felt so privileged and very chastened when I awoke the next morning, and with renewed determination, I got ready for work with a much lighter heart.

Note:
Guides and angels have a profound understanding and never-ending patience, plus a strong sense of humor. They never tire of us because they know us, inside out.

ANGELS OR GUIDES?

People wonder, "Are spiritual guides and angels one and the same?" This is a common misconception. Guides are people in the spiritual realms who have lived on earth, while angels have never had an earthly existence because they are entirely heavenly beings. Consider that, unlike angels, guides have lived on our planet in the past and have individual personalities. Having come up through the ranks, they have evolved into special human beings. They have continued reincarnating until they have gained a form of perfection. Their next step is to become even more knowledgeable in the spirit world, and to dedicate themselves to helping humanity. In this way they can elevate themselves even higher on the ladder of awareness and become nearer to the godhead. After a time, they will become grand masters and mix constantly with the angelic frequencies. Quite a few of my clients report that their guides are Indian, Chinese, Egyptian, and so on. I think the guides create an image of what they looked like in a previous Earth life because it makes it easier for the human brain to connect with a face and form, rather than an intangible entity.

EARTH AVATARS

Selected guides will reincarnate in human form and devote themselves to a person with a particular problem. This is especially so if that person has tried in many past lives to get rid of a bad habit and has not succeeded. By helping the person to resolve it, the avatar earns extra honor and reaches a higher level of consciousness. These guides are called "Earth avatars," and there are many on the planet, even as you read these words.

WHAT IS MY GUIDE'S NAME?

If you meditate for a short time and ask your guide for his or her name before you sleep, you should have the answer when you wake up. Think of the first name that comes into your head, and you will be more or less right. Sometimes your guide will give you special clues. You might hear a name on the radio two or three times in one day, and then again on the television in the evening. Perhaps you might be stuck behind a moving van with the same name emblazoned across the rear of the vehicle, or you might be introduced to someone with that same name. It pays to be observant of the ways of the spiritual world. Angels delight in the synchronicity of three, and when that occurs, you can rely on the information. I am sure you have heard of the old saying "Everything happens in threes!"

HOW MANY GUIDES DO WE HAVE?

We may have two or three guides to aid us through the different stages of our lives. You may wonder why we have guides when an angel will do. I have often wondered this myself, but I believe the guides are dedicated to helping us with our day-to-day problems and that they enjoy interacting with us, especially while we sleep; hence the old saying, "Go to bed with a worry and you will wake up with the answer."

Perhaps the guides are the primary school teachers and the angels are the secondary school teachers. Until we advance spiritually, these loving beings can help bridge the gap for us, and then we will be ready for more communication with the angels.

FAMILY GUIDES

As well as our guides, we may have family members caring for us after they have passed into the spirit world. A beloved husband might make his presence known by moving an object, or an object may even get lost for a day or two, and then reappear in a most unlikely place. A deceased mother might drift her perfume into the room to let us know she is there. When we think about lost loved ones, they immediately tune in to us. Often a family member will intercede for us and ask favors of the spirit world to help us along our way. Our special person might get our attention by stopping a clock and then restarting it again. Family pets might seem preoccupied and unsettled when they sense the presence of "someone" in the room. When this happens, we must try to focus on who has come to visit. A friend of mine once asked, however, "Is it right for us to keep bothering our lost ones? By doing so, we might stop them from moving on."

To some extent I feel she is right. If we cannot stop grieving, it upsets them, and they, in turn, fret about us. The spirit world is very beautiful, and there is much there to interest and occupy our departed friends. If we interfere with them, however, we can hinder them from moving on, learning, and being happy. Therefore, we must strike a balance. We can think of them and the happy memories we shared, but we must also let them move on. After all, the time that we spend on Earth is but the blink of an eye, and then we go back "home" to be reunited with those we love. If our loved ones do choose to come and visit us on occasion, we can assume that the spirit world has given them permission to do so.

4

ANIMALS, HEAVEN, AND ANGELS

WHERE DO ANIMALS
GO WHEN THEY DIE?

When a creature passes into spirit, it reunites with its collective vibration: a feline vibration, a canine vibration, an avian vibration, a bovine vibration, an equine vibration, and so on . . . a place where each species resides in perfect harmony. If they wish to connect with the other animal vibrations, including the human vibration, they can do so.

I believe there is a special plane for them, and once back in the spirit world we can visit them whenever we want. Angels dutifully minister to their needs. If a departed pet should want to visit you, it can do so, especially when it feels the need to bring comfort. It will often stay for quite a while, and you might even catch a magical glimpse of a tail disappearing around the door. I could feel my Siamese cat, George, around me for about two years, and then suddenly he disappeared. No doubt he is now very happy and preoccupied in his new spiritual home.

I remember once awakening slowly from a morning dream in which I had been with my white miniature poodle, which

had died many years before at the grand old age of seventeen. My eyes were still closed when I suddenly felt a warm bundle being put in my arms. I knew it was my dog. I dared not open my eyes, but I cuddled her into me for a few precious moments. When she was alive, she was a busy, wriggly dog that didn't like being held for long periods, but this time she stayed quiet and still, allowing me the privilege of her company. All too soon it was over and I felt her weight lighten and then disappear. Gradually I opened my eyes and looked down into my empty arms. I knew that she had asked to be with me and that the angel of canines had permitted our meeting. Once again I was reassured that all life goes on and that we will be with our loved ones and treasured pets after our time on Earth.

Many stories are told of near-death experiences in which people (particularly children) are greeted by an angel accompanied by a favorite and much-loved pet who has died. The pet comes along to comfort and reassure the visitor.

POWER ANIMAL GUIDES

Power animal guides dwell in a sacred and rarefied environment in the spirit world, but they can become attached to you. They are mentally far superior to other creatures, and they constantly mingle with the angels who care for animals. Our own pets have to evolve when they die, and these fabulous creatures are icons for them to look up to and eventually strive to become. The power animal's role is to guide and protect us on our journey in life. Whatever

strength or talent the creature embodies, it will gladly give to you. A wolf or meerkat will teach us how to react within a close-knit family group. A feline will inspire patience, psychic ability, and independence. A bird represents freedom and will help you to lose your fear of heights. The equine teaches graceful movement and deportment. Are you clumsy in this life? If so, concentrate on the horse vibration. The fabulous unicorn will instruct you on perfect universal love. The unicorn has no dark thoughts—only pure love—and will assist you in reaching a higher, purer vibration.

The animal you favor will be the one that guards you, and if you are in danger, you can ask for its assistance and protection at any time.

A SPECIAL CAT CALLED MERLIN

About six years ago, my husband and I adopted two elderly seal-point Siamese cats. The previous owner had died, and his relatives had placed the animals in a cat sanctuary. Strangely, they had never been named, so they were known only as "the big one" and "the little one." We brought them home, where we had collars already made up for them with their new name tags. After two days, Merlin managed to open the screen door and flee into the fields at the back of our garden. I was horrified. There are

hundreds of acres out there. As he had always been kept inside, he had lost his hunting ability and he would never survive in the open. He was gone for more than twenty-eight days, and my psychic ability showed me that his vital organs were breaking down. He did not know his new name, he did not know our location—or us—and, worst of all, I could feel that he was starving. One particular day, I was in my beautiful conservatory looking anxiously across the garden and wishing fervently that he would come home. My heart was low, so I asked out loud, "Elvenia, angel of animals, please guide Merlin back to the garden." With a sigh I turned away and went into the bathroom to wash my hands and prepare for my next client.

When I went back into the conservatory, a frail and sickly Merlin was standing in the middle of the garden. I was shocked to see how quickly my request had been answered. In time, Merlin recovered.

5

GOOD AND BAD TIMES

ANGELS OF KARMA

The karmic angels make sure that our lessons are fair and that we can cope with whatever we are given in life. At every stage in our lives, they monitor us closely to assess our successes and failures. A few wise old sayings characterize the nature of this relationship:

- You reap what you sow.
- What goes around comes around.
- Be careful of whose toes you stand on when you are on your way up; you could meet them on the way down.

The karmic laws are very strict, so we get away with nothing. There is payback for every negative action. A thought is a powerful living thing, and it can cause good or evil, so we must be careful about the ideas that we have and whom we project them on.

The way we have lived in previous lives bears some responsibility for who we are now and what we have today. The worst offenses a human can perpetrate are murder and cruelty to any living thing. Only the Divine Source has the right to end a life.

SUFFERING PAIN

Although some may find this a controversial subject, many spiritual people believe that before the soul incarnates, it agrees that the person who will embody it should undergo pain and suffering, especially when he or she is young. Angels teach us that pain heals the negative vibration of humankind's evil deeds in previous lifetimes and that it creates a sort of cleansing. An elderly relative of mine once remarked that this might be the reason why childbirth is so painful. Every birthing mother is trying to heal the karmic debts of the past by taking on the excruciating pains of labor. A prime example of intense pain is portrayed in the Christian faith, in which Jesus Christ was brutally tortured and crucified, and then died in agony to save humankind from the previous sins of the world. Many say angels ministered to him throughout the crucifixion.

ANGELS AND SUICIDE

The unfortunate souls who take their own lives are never punished. They receive deep love and understanding from the angelic realms when they return to the spirit world. Initially, the angels of karma take them to a place of beauty and healing so they can be restored to full mental and physical health and balance. It is believed that anyone who takes his or her own life must reincarnate quite quickly to similar parents and family background as before and that the individual must face the same hurdles in life again. There is no way out, but we are told that the angels never give us anything we cannot handle. Although angels are always sympathetic, suicide is severely frowned upon because of the havoc that is left behind and because causing this "offense" adds significantly to the soul's negative karma. Think of the effect that is created with the living children, partners, and parents who are left to pick up the pieces. The grieving, sadness, and tears that can last a lifetime have to be considered, as well as the guilt that so many feel. They ask, "How could we have helped them?" "Could it have been prevented?" "Was it my fault?"

We reincarnate to dispel negative karma, not to add to it!

If you feel that you cannot cope with life, summon an angel to give you the courage and optimism that will get you back on track. If only we could see what was around the next corner, life would not appear to be quite so bleak, and our hearts would be braver. There is always a new day to look forward to, and we must approach life as a sometimes difficult but always exciting journey. Greet the day!

GUARDIAN ANGELS

A guardian angel is a savior who will be present at the eleventh hour. These angels come when we are in grave danger. If fate throws us into the path of disaster and we are in the wrong place at the wrong time (and, most important, if it is not our time to die) they can, by the laws of the cosmos, intervene and save us. The time we are born and the time we die are recorded in the Akashic Records, which are in the spirit realms, so there are usually no mistakes. I have read many angel books in which people have remarked that they were granted a last-minute reprieve from some form of disaster and that they were given help in the most unexpected way. Here are two examples that I have heard myself.

Amrik

At the age of nine, Amrik attended a school outing in the Malvern Hills in Worcester, England. The scenery was ruggedly beautiful and

he was enjoying a quiet stroll among the grassy pathways, admiring the rolling hills and wildflowers. Suddenly his foot slipped on a wet tuft of grass and he staggered forward. He was on a steep slope, so he couldn't stop, and he started to lurch wildly down the hill, completely out of control. He knew there was a vertical drop of 160 feet just ahead of him, and he panicked, trying frantically to stop running. Suddenly he felt a great calmness come over him, and then an unseen hand pushed him to one side, breaking his fall. Lying on his back in astonishment, he knew that an angel had intervened and saved him. I asked him if this act of wonder had changed the way he felt. Amrik said that his faith had been inspired and that the incident had remained with him throughout his life.

The Boat

Ben is a really nice, very athletic young man. I had been doing readings for him for a couple of years and I always enjoyed his open-mindedness. I once remarked when doing a palm reading for him that he had a strong mount of Neptune, which meant that he would never drown. He breathed a great sigh of relief and said that he had always been anxious about drowning. I tried to reassure him and said it was probably a fear created by an experience in a past life.

A year or so went by, and Ben returned for another look into the future. I informed him that he was always protected in moments of danger. After the reading, he told me that a short time earlier he had been in great peril; he had gotten out of his depth while swimming because he had severe cramp, and he couldn't move. All he could see was the waterline in front of his eyes, but he kept reassuring himself that he would never drown. Out of nowhere, a small boat drew up next to him.

In it was a strangely beautiful young woman who smiled serenely at him. He knew she was an angel. She didn't say a word to him, but she encouraged him to put his hand on the boat. She then led him safely to the shore. She disappeared instantly once his feet touched the sand!

CHILDREN'S ANGELS

In Victorian society, it was well-known that little children were under the protection and guardianship of special angels. Spiritually minded people tend to hold this belief even now. I feel in my heart that this is true, and it gives me much comfort. An angel who particularly loves children is Paige, so it is she who will minister to sick or unhappy children. If a request is made to a children's angel, the gift of a baby can be granted to couples who are finding it hard to conceive.

Adele and Mark

Adele and Mark have been clients of mine for many years. Adele e-mailed me one day and seemed very down. She and Mark had been trying unsuccessfully to have a baby for quite some time, and even IVF treatments had not been successful. Adele was worried because her biological clock was running out.

"What can I do, Beleta? Will you do a reading for me and tell me if we are ever going to have this baby?" I thought about my reply to her for quite some time. Suddenly my guide's voice spoke to me: "Tell them to ask an angel." Immediately the angel Paige came into my head. She was, after all, the angel of children, so perhaps she would help Adele and Mark!

With fingers flying over the keyboard, I wrote them an inspired reply. First, I told them to find a flat surface and to put yellow flowers and a picture of a baby on it. I knew Adele loved crystals, so I asked her to place a piece of rose quartz with the other items, as well as a photograph of both of herself and Mark. Then they had to take a small yellow candle and inscribe on it with a pin the words For us, a healthy baby soon.

I told them to light the candle and stand it at the front of their makeshift altar. Together they were to hold hands and say, three times, with as much feeling as they could muster, "Angel Paige, please grant us the privilege of a healthy new baby."

Two months went by, and to be truthful, I didn't give any thought to Adele and Mark because I was so busy. But then one day I opened my e-mail and saw a message from Adele. I read it quickly and gasped. The email said, "Beleta, I am pregnant . . . it actually worked!"

After many years of waiting, their dreams had at last come true. Six months later, Harry was born, hale and hearty, and the joy of his parents was complete. Many people have admired this little boy and remarked, "He's so beautiful; he has the face of an angel."

Those who are cynical might say that it was a coincidence. But I know in my heart that Paige had really answered their prayers. Although rose quartz is not the crystal that is usually linked to Paige, it is the right one for the purpose of encouraging fertility, so in this case, I decided to bend the rules and to use it. Sometimes one has to do what feels right rather than follow the rules.

Leanna

Leanna Greenaway is the author of *Simply Tarot*, *Practical Spellcraft*, and *Simply Wicca*. She is my daughter, and I feel, as every parent does about his or her child, that she is special. From an early age, as young as three years old, she showed a remarkable spiritual side. To some extent over the years, she has educated her mother in holistic and esoteric matters, or perhaps reminded me of what I had long forgotten! I did not dwell on guides, angels, life after death, or reincarnation until I became her mother in my early twenties.

Unfortunately, as a child, Leanna suffered intense ear infections and practically lived on antibiotics. She was forever at the doctor's office and seeing specialists, but they could do little to help in those days. One evening, when she was about three years old, I went to check on her and found her sitting cross-legged on her bed. With her eyes closed tightly, her little face was tilted upward in intense concentration. She looked so beautiful and ethereal, with her long dark brown hair tumbling over her shoulders, that I did not want to disturb her. After a few moments, she opened her eyes and looked at me.

"What are you doing? Why aren't you asleep?" I asked.

"My ears were hurting so much, Mummy, so I asked the angels to take the pain away."

"And did they?" I responded with surprise.

She nodded fervently. "Yes, pain all gone now."

Later, when she was asleep, I thought about her words and wondered how she knew to ask an angel for help. I had never given her any guidance about them; we were not even churchgoers.

HEALING ANGELS

If we ask for assistance when a member of our family or one of our friends is not well, help will be given. Miracles can occur when a healing angel intervenes. The power of prayer is very potent, and it teaches us how to focus and draw the angels to us. It has been known that after prayer, cancer will sometimes go into remission, and tumors will shrink and disappear, with the help of the Divine Being and the angels.

6

MEDITATION

YOUR MEDITATION

Lie comfortably on your back with a pillow under your knees. If you have some beautiful soft music, play it to help you relax. You don't want the music to stop and interrupt the flow of your meditation, so set the player to repeat. Close your eyes and breathe deeply for about two minutes. Concentrate on the sound of your breathing, bringing the air through your nose and drawing the breaths fully and slowly from your lower stomach into your chest. Repeat this process over and over again. You will find that you will naturally lengthen your breathing pattern and get into your own rhythm. Let your mind wander, and just get used to what you are doing. You can remain in this state for about twenty minutes, or longer, if you want.

Focus on your third eye, the place just above the bridge of your nose or in between your eyebrows. As you continue to breathe deeply, in your mind the area of the third eye will appear like a dark television screen, spread across your forehead. Gaze out of this as far as you can. This process will take practice and patience. Sometimes it may take you two or three attempts before you get it right. Ask your angel to connect with you. You might say something as simple as, "Angel, can we have a chat?"

In your mind, focus on a beautiful carved wooden door.
Approach it and knock; then wait for it to open. You should
still be breathing fully and slowly; now try to deepen your
breathing even more. You will see a golden light appear as
the door opens a little. Push the door open and step into the
light. Take a good look around. You are in the most fabulous
garden, with flowers that you have never seen before and
colors that are more vivid and brilliant than any you have
seen on Earth. Invite your angel to join you on the bench.
Now you can ask for guidance, protection, love, or whatever
else you need.

7

ANGELS IN RELIGION

ISLAM

The religion of Islam ascribes huge importance to the angels, who were known as mala'ika in Arabic. The mala'ika were believed to be invisible entities created by the Divine Being to serve on important assignments. The most elevated was Jibra'il (Gabriel) who was traditionally known to be the mediator between God and the Prophet Mohammed, at the time when the Koran was first revealed to humankind.

The Koran says that each of us has two angels. One is a guardian and the other records our sins and achievements while we are on Earth.

THE FOUR MAJOR ISLAMIC ANGELS

Jibra'il (Gabriel)

The archangel Jibra'il was the principal of the angels; he communicated with all the prophets in the Muslim religion. The Koran specifically mentions him and reveres him at the highest level.

Azra'il (Azrael)

Known as the Angel of Death, Azra'il and his helpers take charge of separating the soul from the human body before it enters the spirit world. If you had the misfortune to have led a dissolute life, then the soul is extracted in the most horrendous way. However, if you have led a blameless life, the soul is taken in a gentle and caring manner.

Mika'il (Michael)

The angel Mika'il is also mentioned in the Koran. He is responsible for bringing storms and thunder and lightning to Earth. His second title is the Angel of Reward, as he is in charge of meting out to us what we deserve.

Israfil (Raphael)

The angel Israfil is mentioned in the Koran. He is the angel who will blow the mighty trumpet on Judgment Day to signal the end of the world. He is also known as the master of music and the patron saint of travelers.

LESSER ISLAMIC ANGELS

Munkar and Nakeer

The two angels Munkar and Nakeer examine the departed person's life and analyze his or her deeds while the person is still in the grave.

Malik

Malik is responsible for the control and management of Hell.

Ridwan

Ridwan is responsible for the management of Paradise.

AN INTERESTING
CONNECTION

Islamic angels seem to come from earlier sources, including Judaism and Christianity, but there is also evidence of something older. The religions of Babylon and Chaldea were formed over ten thousand years ago and their priests were also astrologers.

Interestingly, the Islamic "Throne Bearer" angels take the form of a Bull, a Lion, an Eagle, and a Man, and these images correspond to the four fixed signs of the zodiac, which are Taurus the Bull, Leo the Lion, Scorpio (with its ancient symbol) the Eagle, and finally, Aquarius, a male figure that later became the Water Bearer. It's also fascinating to consider that these four figures are also depicted on the ceiling of the central dome of St. Peter's in the Vatican.

JUDAISM

The Jewish teachings on angels (mal'ach), or "messengers," as they are sometimes known, refer back to the first five books of the Torah in the Old Testament. Many stories are recorded of angelic intervention and help. In the book of Genesis, Jophiel cast Adam and Eve out of the Garden of Eden, and from that day forth, the cherubim have guarded the gates of Eden so no man or woman can enter.

Many of the Jewish angels are similar to the Christian angels and frequently hold the same names and titles. Some medieval Jewish scholars suggest that the angels' role is to execute issues that are beneath the dignity of the Divine Being, thus allowing the Creator a more distant approach. In the Old Testament, biblical angels fulfill a variety of roles, such as smiting the enemies of Israel, not to mention protecting and shielding humankind. Angels passed on information and messages from the Almighty, so fear and awe went hand in hand when these powerful mysterious creatures appeared.

The angels Michael, Uriel, Raphael, and Gabriel protect humankind during the sleeping hours, and these four angels, one at each corner of the bed, will ward off any evil. They can also be summoned to help a student learn and memorize the Torah.

All Jewish angels do not have gender in the human sense but are given a masculine aspect and carry male names.

CHRISTIANITY AND RELIGIOUS ANGELS

There are many references to angelic beings in the scriptures, though there seems to be no specific date as to when they were first created. Some say that they came into existence after God had completed his task of creating the Earth. The Bible says that there are millions of angels whose role is ministering to humankind. The word "angel" comes from the Greek word "angelos," meaning "messenger." The word "angel" is mentioned 108 times in the Old Testament and 165 times in the New Testament. In Christianity, angels have no flesh or bones, as they are beings of light and energy, although they can be in only one place at a time. The scriptures teach us that angels are not omniscient, but I am sure they know a lot more than we do!

The following is a selection of Christian and religious angels.

Cassiel, or Kafziel

Cassiel is an angel of temperance who can provide assistance with mind expansion and memory. He is said to be fond of dragons, but his main role is to watch over the planet Saturn. Also known as the Angel of Tears and Tribulations, he is the leader of the choir of angels known in the Bible as "the powers."

Chamuel

The angel Chamuel (He Who Seeks God) gave Christ strength in the garden of Gethsemane. He is renowned for his compassion and communication skills and is said to inspire art and beauty. He is sometimes known as the Angel of Karma.

Gabriel

The angel Gabriel (God Is My Strength) sits on the left-hand side of the Creator. Some scholars say that Gabriel is female, and many artistic masters have created this image, especially as Gabriel is linked to pregnancy and fertility. He or she visited Zacharias and told him that his wife, Elizabeth, was soon to have a child, John the Baptist (Luke 1:11–20). The angel Gabriel also foretold the birth of Jesus Christ. Gabriel is thought to be a bringer of good news, and in iconic paintings he is depicted blowing a large golden trumpet. Although he made only four appearances in the Bible, the angel Gabriel is one of the best-known angels in Christianity.

Metatron

Metatron is the supreme angel of death, an enormous being of brilliant hues and light, the most elevated of all angels. He is said to be the king of the angels and is often depicted with the scroll of knowledge in his outstretched hand. Thus he is known as the Scribe of God and the Angel of the Covenant.

He was traditionally known as the prophet Enoch, who ascended into Heaven and was transformed into the Angel of Fire, with thirty-six wings.

Sandalphon

Sandalphon is the mighty twin brother of Metatron; he is usually depicted as lofty and majestic. Attired in black from head to toe, he makes an imposing figure. His prime role is to fight the powers of Satan, or the Prince of Darkness. Formerly known as the prophet Elias, he is summoned to help us gain spiritual knowledge. On a lighter note, he is the master of melodic tunes and lyrics. Perhaps he assists the composers of our world with their work.

Michael

Michael is one of the most popular and beloved of the archangels, as he is the Angel of Protection and the celestial commander of God's army. He is shown with a mighty sword in his hand, ready to smite the enemy and wreak vengeance and destruction. He is often depicted in armor and is beautiful to behold . . . a pinup of the angelic world! He cast Satan out of Heaven and is known as the Defender of the Faith. His job is to weigh the souls of the dead on Judgment Day.

Raphael

The angel Raphael (God Has Healed) is the healer and pro-
tector of the innocent and the young. His eyes penetrate the
entire universe and see all that is wrong. He misses nothing.
Christians invoke this angel for a miracle cure, especially at
the eleventh hour. If someone in a family is suffering, he is
the angel to call upon. He is often linked with travel and
safety. If you are feeling off-color, Raphael will help; just ask
him! He is one of my favorite angels.

Uriel

Uriel (Fire of God) has many titles: Angel of Music, Angel of
Poetry and Verse, and Angel of Psychic Vision and Nature. If
requested, he will talk to you in dream sleep and help with
any problems you may have. This beautiful angel will inspire
art projects and psychic abilities.

Fire transforms and is powerful, so Uriel is often depicted
with a burning flame in his outstretched hand. He brings
the flame of love to all humankind. Uriel was the angel
messenger who gave Noah advice and warning about the
Great Flood.

Jophiel

Jophiel (Beauty of God) is the first angel mentioned in the Bible. His role is to guard the Tree of Life for the Creator. Grasping a fearsome, fiery sword, he had the awesome task of banishing Adam and Eve from the Garden of Eden, and will deter any human from stepping onto the hallowed ground again. He has wisdom, will give inspiration, and will help you to use discrimination.

Zadkiel

Zadkiel (Righteousness of God) is also known as Zachiel or Zidekiel and is one of the seven archangels. Many pictures and paintings depict him with a small dirk, or dagger, in his hand. He is renowned for ruling over and guarding the planet Jupiter. Modern teachings lean toward him helping with our spiritual development and the power of prayer. This angel assists Michael as a sort of second lieutenant in battle.

Raguel

Raguel (Friend of God) is one of the seven archangels and is known as the Angel of Ice and Snow. It is said that he will call forth the other angels on the Day of Judgment. In today's world, we would liken him to a lawyer, bringing fairness to unjust circumstances. His main role is to keep the other angels in order.

Hanael, or Anael

The angel Hanael (Grace of God) holds the title of the Prince of the Angelic Orders or the Angel of Principalities and Virtues. As one of the seven archangels, he is honored and revered on the highest level. Some say Hanael is an androgynous angel, neither male nor female. He or she will bring love and harmony to the home, and sustain friendships. Dressed in colors of verdant green, with pale dove gray wings and carrying a lantern to show us the way, this angel strikes an imposing figure.

8

THE ANGELIC
HIERARCHY

Throughout the ages, the church and scholars have come to the conclusion that angels are divided into different ranks, or clans, and that they have individual duties to perform for humankind and the universe. No one is quite sure about how many orders exist—some say nine, others twelve.

THE NINE ORDERS (OR CHOIRS) OF ANGELS

- The seraphim
- The cherubim
- The thrones
- The dominions
- The virtues
- The powers
- The principalities
- The archangels
- The angels

The Seraphim

The leader of the seraphim (also known as fire makers or fiery serpents) is Uriel. The seraphim love music and sing constantly. They are often depicted in iconic paintings and works of art with long golden trumpets, uplifted in worship of the Creator. These wonderful beings of such intense light and radiance often dazzle the lesser angels, who find it uncomfortable even to gaze at them. The seraphim regulate the heavenly movements and pass the light of the divine to the lower ranks of angels and creatures of our world.

The Cherubim

The principal of the cherubim (which means "full of knowledge") is Jophiel. The cherubim are the college graduates of the heavenly realms; they have unlimited knowledge and divine wisdom. One of their main tasks is to make sure all universal laws are obeyed. Karma is high on their list of priorities, and any action that humans incur or project toward another will always have good or bad influences returned on them. The cherubims' judgments are fair, and they inspire others to spiritual renewal and remind us of the laws of cause and effect.

The Thrones

The leader of the thrones (also called the "ophanim") is Japhkiel. The thrones are the peacemakers; they deliver harmony to all negative situations. They can bridge gaps between the visible and invisible worlds, bringing spiritual perfection and divinity to the universe. They are impartial and strictly fair, but also humble in their service to humankind.

The seraphim, the cherubim, and the thrones, collectively, are the first triad, or trinity, of angels.

The Dominions

The principal of the dominions is Zadkiel. The dominions work mainly in the spirit realms, seldom interfering with earthly matters. Sometimes they are referred to as "flashing swords." They are responsible for ensuring that the universal laws move in perfection and for unifying and overseeing the more junior angels.

The Virtues

The leader of the virtues (sometimes known as the brilliant ones) is Hanael. The virtues are radiant with resplendent colors that dazzle those that behold them. One of their many duties is to give courage and compassion to humans, sometimes giving a gentle push to get us up the hill. They are known to create miracles, so they are sometimes called the bestowers. They keep an eye on nature and make sure that the crops grow.

The Powers

The head of the powers (sometimes called the "lightning swords") is Raphael. These angels ward off evil or sinister spirits and defend the weak and unprotected. They will help you to stick up for yourself in an argument or in situations of confrontation. They will protect and defend against anyone who tries to overthrow the universal laws and the divine plans.

The dominions, the virtues, and the powers make up the second tier of the angelic realms.

The Principalities

The principalities (also called the "worldly guides") have to set a good example for the lesser angels. You can think of them as the senior boys and senior girls of the angelic realms because their standards are very high. Their main task is to watch over our planet and its people, towns, and cities. These angels are multinational guardians of our globe. If you are unsure of where you are traveling to, or if you have a difficult journey and get lost, shout for these angels and they should get you to your destination without too much hassle. They have a strong humanitarian instinct and they understand us totally. They have a great sense of humor too!

The Seven Archangels (Celestial Envoys)

The names of the seven archangels differ in different biblical accounts; nevertheless, the following are commonly recognized names of these archangels:

- Michael
- Uriel
- Gabriel
- Raphael
- Hanael
- Zadkiel
- Raguel

These seven emissaries, the archangels, have special prominence, and they are the best known of the angelic groups, as many people all over the world recognize their names. They have specific duties and assignments to help humankind achieve a better understanding of life and values. Some are healers, others protectors and coordinators. The archangels concern themselves with the human world; they are here to be of service to us. They do not consider themselves any better than us, so if you do summon angels of the universe, they must attend you by the laws of the cosmos. Each and every one of them has a guardianship role.

The principalities, the archangels, and the angels make up the third and last tier of the angelic realms.

HELL'S ANGELS

Religion teaches us that the angels of hell are "fallen angels," or angels that have become arrogant and proud. The scriptures say that the Creator had great compassion for them and that he would allow them to climb the ladder toward purity if they repented. In the teachings of the Bible, these fallen angels were sent to hell to mix with devils and demons in the underworld.

9

MORE ANGELS

DAILY ANGELS

There are millions of angels that minister to the human race. They are often called "daily angels," and they can help with little tasks that seem complicated or annoying to us.

Not so long ago, a small wren flew into my conservatory and was crashing about among the flowers and plants. The bird was obviously petrified, and after fifteen minutes or so, totally exhausted. As I have two Siamese cats, I was anxious to make sure I rescued the bird, but it kept evading me and flopped behind various flowerpots. In exasperation, I called out, "Angels, can you get this little bird out of here, please?" Within seconds, the wren flew straight down along the length of the conservatory and out through the doorway into the bright sunshine.

I often ask the angels for help if I am doing a crossword puzzle and get stuck on a clue, or perhaps when I need a parking space, or even when I'm trying to thread a needle. Angels love to be of assistance in even the smallest way, and nothing is too mundane for them. Why not experiment?

ANGELS OF THE SEASONS

Spring

Raphael is known as a wonderful healer; he is the guardian of springtime. His job is to watch over the crops, tend the seeds, and prepare the earth, especially if it has been ravaged by fire, flood, or famine. He nurtures new growth and has strong associations with the Tree of Life. Sometimes if I have a sick houseplant, I will ask him to help it to return to health again.

Summer

Uriel helps to make the blossoms form, plants to burst into bloom, and grain to swell. He is also the angel of music, song, and karmic laws. As the old saying goes, "You reap what you sow!

Autumn

Michael helps those who tend the land, such as farmers, who plough the fields and grow and harvest barley and wheat. He is the angel of gardeners and provides strength and stamina for physical labor and toil. As he is a harvest angel, country folk hold him in high esteem.

Winter

Gabriel is connected with the wintertime. He helps to heal and nurture the ground before the next new upsurge of growth in the springtime. He brings harmony, balance, and good news for a productive outcome when he is summoned. He is also known as the angel of hope.

SHAPE-CHANGING ANGELS

Angels can alter their shape and appearance in the blink of an eye. They can be huge enough to fill a skyline or small enough to fit in the palm of a hand. They can be found in every country in the world, and their appearance and nationality will blend with those of the people that they meet in the various countries where they find themselves. All angels are beatific to behold, but they can sometimes take on the guise of ordinary human beings who might be sitting next to us on a train or a bus. Children's angels will ensure that they don't look threatening, so they can appear as little ones themselves. They reassure and soothe youngsters, often leading them out of danger. Angels can also create images of themselves in wallpaper, fabrics, mists, or clouds. Everything is possible: they really are among us!

Justin

Twenty-year-old Justin was in a bar having a drink with one of his friends. His friend had just gone to the restroom, and Justin was looking forward to meeting up with some other friends later that evening. As he quietly sipped his beer, an unknown assailant came out of nowhere and in an unprovoked attack punched Justin's glass straight into his face. Shards of glass embedded in his skin and blood spurted everywhere as the man ran off. Later that night, after returning from the hospital, Justin looked down at his blue-and-white-checked shirt. On his shirt, exactly on the spot that lay over his heart, was a bloodstain that made a perfect image of a small angel. Although the attack was very distressing, Justin realized that it could have been so much worse if he had not had the protection of his special angel. He has kept the shirt as a reminder of the episode.

ANGEL FEATHERS (THE ANGELS' CALLING CARDS)

Some would say that my family is very superstitious, especially about feathers, and I will personally acknowledge this. Feathers are from birds, and birds are messengers! The North American Indians used eagle feathers to adorn their headdresses and costumes, not to mention their dream catchers! If you see a particular white feather in your pathway, pick it up because it will be a message from the angels for you.

Here are two stories connected with feathers.

I am not a very good traveler and I worry about getting on planes, preferring to keep at least one foot on the ground. Each time I travel, I wait for a white feather to appear from the angels to tell me that I will be safe, and usually one makes an appearance! I remember, before a trip to Russia, seeing a small white feather lying on the carpet in my living room. It had not been there the night before, so how did it get there? On another occasion, we were in an elevator in the Chicago airport prior to flying, and there was a white feather on the floor right in front of our eyes. Coincidence? I think not!

Before another trip, when my husband and I were due to fly to Austria, no white feathers had appeared, and I was getting really worried. What if we crashed going over the Austrian Alps? My husband, who is more down-to-earth than I am, glared over his small round spectacles and told me to stop being a drama queen. "Do you want to ruin the holiday before we even get there?" he remonstrated sternly.

The following day, I had just three readings to do. My last client was Patricia. As she sat down, she fumbled in her spacious handbag and handed me a long white envelope.

"These are for you, Beleta," she said. "I found them by the riverbank when I was out walking yesterday. I thought you might like them."

Inside were three perfect white swan's feathers. I could

have kissed her! Needless to say, later on, when I showed them to my husband, he raised his eyebrows and shook his head in wonderment.

On another occasion, we had saved for three years to visit the Canadian Rockies and to take an Alaskan cruise. I was unsettled and, strangely, not looking forward to it. Nothing my husband or my family said could cheer me up. With only four days left until our departure, I still had not bothered to pack. My mood was so black, I could not lift it. I asked my guide to inspire me or at least inform me of what was about to happen. But no information came, and neither did any reassuring feathers. Then my husband came in beaming from the garden. He had a large tail feather in his hand. "Look! Your feather has appeared. It was on the conservatory doorstep, so now you can stop worrying and get your packing done."

It was a magpie's feather and very beautiful with its shimmering colors of blue and green. But my heart sank like a stone, because traditional folklore tells us that magpies are messengers of doom, disaster, and death.

The day before we were to travel, the awful tragedy of the World Trade Center happened and Canadian air space was closed!

Now I knew why my mood had been so bleak. To our huge disappointment, we canceled the trip. The following year, we took the trip and had the most amazing holiday. Did I get the white feathers from my angels beforehand? Well, of course I did!

BABY FEATHERS

In my job, I meet many interesting people. One regular client told me a fascinating story about her daughter. After Jenny's reading, she told me that her girl had suffered quite a few miscarriages and despaired of ever carrying a child to term. One day while on vacation, they were both lying on the beach sunning themselves in their bikinis. Her daughter, who was four months pregnant, turned to Jenny and said, "Mom do you think I will carry this child full term?" Out of nowhere, a little white feather drifted down and landed in the girl's naval. Jenny said she knew it was a message from the angels, who were reassuring her daughter that the baby would be wonderful—and, of course, he was!

ANGELIC WARNING!

When my daughter was about eight or nine, her passion was dancing, and she competed in different dancing festivals across the north of England. On one particular day, her father and I set off in the car with her to a destination some fifty miles away. It was going to be a long day, and we would not be returning until around midnight. We had gone only a hundred yards up the road when a gentle angelic voice spoke in my ear, saying, "Turn the car around and go back to the house. Something is very wrong."

I said to my husband, "Quick—go back to the house immediately!" He did not argue but turned the car around right
away. We pulled up outside our home and my husband
rushed in to find a burglar just smashing the glass panes of
our kitchen window. The intruder fled empty-handed. Unfortunately, we could not catch him and so he was never pros-
ecuted. Even so, I felt protected by the angels, especially as
we would have been out all day and, if they hadn't warned
us, our treasured possessions would have been taken and
our home turned upside down.

10

MODERN ANGELS

I have mentioned in other chapters that there are thousands, if not millions, of angels in service to humankind. The religious or traditional angels that are mentioned in the Bible and other books will always have their place in our culture and beliefs, but we must also introduce a newer vibration of angels to help with the day-to-day problems that we encounter. The information for these newer angels, listed below, was channeled to me and to some of my soul sisters many years ago from the spirit world, and I am grateful that they have given me the opportunity to share it with you. I feel in a way that this is divine providence.

You can perform a small ritual and use an angel altar that you can set up for each angel. This is important and will help you to focus yourself for prayer. Sometimes the elements you include on your altar will have to be adapted for different angels.

THE ANGEL ALTAR

It is best to be well prepared when you wish to connect with an angel, especially if you want to ask the angel to do you a favor. Try to have a small altar set up at all times if you can, and keep some of the elements listed below on hand. This will be your sacred place that will allow you to focus on angelic connection; please do not allow others to infringe upon this space.

Your altar will probably fascinate your children, so let them make a little one of their own (minus the candles and incense, for safety's sake).

Preparing Your Altar

You will need the following items:

- A small table or shelf (even the top
  of a chest of drawers will do)
- A cloth in a soft pastel color
- Fresh or silk flowers
- Crystals
- Small, thin pastel candles
- A picture of an angel
- A picture of you
- Any white or pretty feathers you have found
- Incense
- A pair of Tibetan bells or a small hand bell

Once these items have been arranged, light a stick of lavender incense and waft it over the altar and around the room; then return it to the altar and place it in a secure holder. Ring the bells three or four times in the air over the altar. Replace them on the altar. Close your eyes and ask aloud for the altar space to be made sacred and pure. Leave the room, closing the door behind you, for at least an hour. When you return, all negative influences will have been cleansed from the room. You will immediately notice a different, lighter vibration in the room.

Note:
Many high churches swing incense around the interior of the church to cleanse it of negative vibrations, while church bells are used for calling the faithful to prayer.

WHY DOES RITUAL WORK?

Nowadays, we seem to have lost the art of ritual, while our ancestors were wiser and more in tune with this important element in their lives. Some traditional churches and religious sects still practice the art of ritual, but they may also need to update their procedures. Ritual teaches us to focus the mind on one thing and not to be distracted by everyday upsets in our lives. Angelic ritual is important, as these beings want your complete attention to be focused on what you are doing, so that you can make the communication and prayer work.

Although few people make a point of practicing a ritual, they often do so unconsciously in several ways. For example, when entering a church, most of us will light a candle and say a prayer. Making a wish before we blow out the candles out on a birthday cake is another favorite. There are special rituals for weddings and christenings, for funerals and baptisms. Singing the school anthem is a form of ritual that creates a feeling of unity and camaraderie, as does psalm singing and chanting in monasteries and convents. Even in this modern age, the crowd at a soccer match enacts group bonding with chanting and singing—and interestingly, some crowds sing what could be termed hymns.

PRAYER

I feel that we are only visitors to this planet for a very short time before we go back to our true home in the spirit world. For some souls it can be hard to be here, and at times it can be extremely lonely. The Earth is used as a schoolroom, and we progress more rapidly by coming here than we do by staying in the exquisite spiritual realms. By using prayer, we connect to those who we knew when we were still in the spirit world, before our current incarnation, especially the divine and our guides and angels. Prayer focuses the mind, raises our vibration, and reminds us of who we really are and what our purpose is here. Through prayer we are reconnecting with our spiritual family, who will keep us centered and on track, especially when we feel desolate and are suffering.

ANGELS AND CANDLES

Throughout history, flame and fire have been revered, and ancient people worshipped and feared the Sun. Without light, our world would be a bleak and dismal place, so people have always valued illumination. When we light a candle, it is a brand-new light that imitates the light of the Creator. The spirit world is ablaze with color and luminosity, so it's not surprising that all the major religions use candles as a part of their rituals and beliefs. Using candles on an angelic altar enhances the prayer aspect and makes the procedure unique to the person who is praying. Candles of different colors and fragrances can also heighten the mood for special entreaties. It is a good idea to have a stock of various colored candles in your home if you become serious about angelic prayer. Keeping them in a special box protects them from negative energies. Handmade candles are better than mass-produced ones, if you can get them.

ANGELS AND CRYSTALS

Crystals are magical minerals that have been a part of our planet from the beginning of time, and they hold many mysteries and the powers of healing. Therefore, if you want to pray to an angel of healing on behalf of a loved one, it would be best to place a healing crystal on the altar, and a good choice would be an amethyst.

If we feel unprotected or fearful of someone, we could use a turquoise crystal, as it wards off negative energy. If we feel lonely and unloved, a citrine will rebalance us. The citrine is often called "the cuddle stone."

Note:
Before using a new crystal, it is best to cleanse it in tepid salt water, dry it, and leave in the sunshine for a few hours to cast off any negative vibrations.

Angel's Hair: Rutile Quartz

Rutile quartz is the most abundant mineral on Earth; it can be found in the United States, Norway, Australia, and Brazil. It is a type of titanium ore that occurs within granite, and it has fine strands of titanium needles embedded in it. When held to the light, the pin-shaped inclusions look multidimensional and golden, hence the name "angel's hair." People born under the sign of Gemini or Taurus should be attracted to this stone, as it is linked with their birth signs. Other varieties of rutile quartz have different colors of angel's hair embedded in them.

Rutile quartz can be used to connect with the angelic realms, and its powerful amplifiers will release blocked energies in the etheric and physical bodies. Many healers use this crystal to balance and align the chakras (points of physical or spiritual energy in the human body). When working on a client, they will use this crystal to cleanse the patient's aura of negativity.

Spiritually, angel's hair can promote the gift of channeling and psychic abilities, enabling one to connect to a higher consciousness and to reach the angelic realms. This little treasure is a must for dream work and astral traveling, and it should be placed under your pillow at night, as it should evoke powerful spiritual dreams. It will also help you to put anything painful that has happened behind you and allow for a newer vibration to enter and start the healing process. I sometimes recommend this crystal to my clients who feel under psychic attack or who are experiencing a strange energy in their house that needs clearing. If a home is haunted or forlorn, rutile quartz is a powerful aid that will lead a lost soul back into the spirit world and usher in angelic care and protection.

If you are feeling depressed or exhausted, keep a piece of rutile quartz in your pocket for a few days. If you are female, place a small piece of the quartz in your bra or as near to your heart chakra as possible. It is a great mineral for lifting the spirits and putting the spring back in your step. If you have a loved one who is under stress or unhappy, the gift of angel's hair should help to restore the balance.

I remember many years ago when a client gave me a small round cabochon of angel's hair. As she dropped it into my hand, I felt a tiny but significant electrical buzz in the middle of my palm. I knew it was powerful and I could not understand why I had not heard of it before. I wasted no time in researching rutile quartz in every crystal book I could lay my hands on. All those years ago we did not have the Internet to help us, so it took quite a while to gather the information. Since that time it has been one of my favorite crystals, especially as it is linked to the angels!

ANGELS AND FLOWERS

In the past, the messages of flowers were passed down from generation to generation, but sadly I feel we have lost much of this information. The Victorians knew a great deal about the subject. We can see this in Victorian drawings and romantic jewelry that contains hidden messages (violets for love; red roses for passion; lilies for sadness and funerals; lavender for peace and healing; and poppies for remembrance). And then there are shamrocks, heather, and four-leaf clovers for good luck and good fortune. The Chinese, for example, link chrysanthemums with funerals. Some thought must go into which flowers to use on the angelic altar. If the prayer is for a child, then primroses, daffodils, or any yellow flower could be used. If your partner is the focus of your attention for prayer, pink roses or violets would be appropriate. Silk flowers are acceptable if you cannot find the fresh ones you need for your altar.

ANGELS AND FEATHERS

Feathers have been mentioned before in this book, and believers in angels know that a white feather is a "calling card" or gift from the angels. Placing feathers on your altar is a compliment to the angelic realms and shows deep respect and devotion. As feathers come from birds, and birds are spiritual messengers, we look on our angels as divine messengers for us.

ANGELS AND INCENSE

Incense is used as a purifier, especially in Asian countries. It cleanses the space we are working in. Each perfume creates its own mood to enhance the ritual of angelic prayer. If someone has been in your house that you do not particularly like, then light some incense and waft it around the room to get rid of their energy. Poppy (opium), or hydrangea incense is particularly useful for this, and it smells wonderful. Jasmine is powerful, as it wards off negativity, and lavender incense is a good multipurpose scent that will help with most situations.

ANGELS' AROMA

I wonder whether any of you have ever experienced the aroma of angels. Mostly, this odd phenomenon occurs just after the death of a beloved. The place you are in fills with a sweet cloying perfume of flowers, and it is unmistakably spiritual, as we do not have that variety of scent in our world. Angels create this scent to show the grieving family that the deceased has arrived safely in the garden of God.

11

HOW TO PRAY IN
THE MODERN WAY

PAIGE, THE ANGEL OF CHILDREN

Altar Accessories

Candle: Yellow, blue, or pink

Crystal: Chalcedony, coral, or topaz

Flower: Daisy or primrose

Herb: Clover

Incense oil: Jasmine

Prayer day: Friday

Feathers: blue or pink

Something personal that belongs to the
    child, such as clothing or favorite toys

Lock of the child's hair

Photograph of the child

Baby tooth (if you have one)

School report

Piece of paper with an example of the
    child's writing or artwork

Paige will help with

- Sibling harmony
- Schoolwork
- Hobbies
- Success with exams
- Bullying
- Confidence
- Social skills and manners
- Difficult behavior
- Sleep problems or night waking

- Crying babies
- Eating disorders
- Support with divorcing parents
- Prevention against pedophilia

Paige is the custodian of children from birth to age sixteen. She is one of the leading angels in the spirit realms, and her sole vocation is to guide the younger generation forward safely in life. As parents we cannot always be with our children, so Paige will come if we need protection for them. When you invoke Paige, she can help in all sorts of ways.

Once you are happy with the way the altar is set up, close your eyes and ask Paige to hear your particular request. Make sure you really mean it; otherwise, it will not work.

ELVENIA, THE ANGEL OF ANIMALS

Altar Accessories
Candle: Orange or white
Crystal: Lazulite
Flower: Pansy
Herb: Vanilla
Incense: Lavender
Prayer day: Saturday
Some of the animal's fur
The animal's collar or lead
Photograph of the animal, the animal's brush,
    or a favorite toy

Elvenia will help with

- Barking dogs
- Snapping dogs
- Bad hygiene
- Lost animals
- Cruelty
- Sick or injured pets
- Patience
- Introducing new pets to established ones
- Prayers for all the animals in the world
- Threatened species
- Thanking animals for food and clothing

Anyone who has owned a pet knows that each creature is unique, having his or her own personality. Pets bring great joy to many, especially the lonely, the elderly, and children.

Summon Elvenia to help sick animals, animals that are troublesome, or those who have been brutalized by humans. You might know of someone who has been ill-treating an animal, but you can do nothing personally to help. Invoke Elvenia through prayer to bring a better life to the unfortunate creature. If you have a pet that soils in your home, Elvenia can restore the balance.

SETH, THE ANGEL OF WAR AND STRIFE

Altar Accessories

Candle: Magenta or white

Crystal: Bloodstone

Flowers: Red poppy

Herb: Columbine or yarrow

Incense: Rose or geranium

Prayer day: Sunday

Feather: white

Picture of the person who needs to be protected

Item belonging to the person who needs to be
protected; for example, a watch or a ring

Seth will help with

- War and fighting
- The armed forces
- The police force
- Controlling teenage gangs
- Violent behavior or bullying
- Cruelty
- Difficult neighbors
- Family feuds

Most humans think of war and death with trepidation, but remember that the beautiful and compassionate angel Seth will, when summoned, help to protect those in battle. If you have loved ones in the armed forces, warring families, or unkind neighbors, or if you live in a violent neighborhood, you can invoke Seth to alleviate the aggravations and bring back peace and harmony. He is especially helpful when domestic violence is terrorizing the home.

IDALINA, THE ANGEL OF ABUNDANCE

Altar Accessories

Candle: Green

Crystal: Quartz

Flower: Yellow poppy (papaver)

Herb: Marjoram

Incense: Honeysuckle

Prayer day: Monday

Money, either coins or notes

Idalina will help with

- A new job
- Success with self-employment
- Good work relationships
- Financial rewards
- Promotions
- Working abroad

In life we work to eat and survive. You are one of the lucky ones if you have a job that you are content with, but many people are stuck in mundane employment and wish the hours away until they can go home. Idalina can help you find a happier and more rewarding atmosphere within your work environment, and hopefully a promotion or a new job will be on the horizon for you. It is no sin to want a little extra money for yourself and your family. Although I am English and have an American father, I sometimes feel that the English frown upon the successful, so I am more inclined to believe the American philosophy, that work and success bring well-deserved rewards. As long as you put in a good day's employment, enjoy your success. Spend a little. Save a little. Give away a little. Money after all is just energy; we will not be frowned upon if we use it wisely.

SHIANNA, THE ANGEL OF ROMANTIC LOVE

Altar Accessories
Flower: Red rose or jasmine
Candle: Pink
Crystal: Aquamarine or rose quartz
Prayer day: Friday
Herb: Cumin
Incense: Jasmine
Red glass heart and red ribbons
Picture of your beloved

Shianna will help with

- Choosing the right partner
- Happiness in marriage

- Blessing a wedding
- Attracting a partner
- Unrequited love
- Reconciliation in love
- Sexual harmony

Love definitely makes the world go around. Where would we be without it? How wonderful it is to have a romantic soul mate; sadly, it is not always easy to find our soul mates. There are more divorces now than ever before, and each of us could have one or even two failed marriages. Shianna, the angel of love and marriage, will help through prayer to bring more understanding, love, and balance to your relationship. If you wish to meet your soul mate, use Shianna to guide you toward that special someone.

ALTHEA, THE ANGEL OF HEALTH AND HEALING

Altar Accessories
Candle: Lavender

Crystal: Amethyst

Flower: Lavender

Herb: Chamomile

Incense: Lavender

Prayer day: Thursday

Picture of the sick person

Something that belongs to the sick person

Althea will help with

- Energy
- Healing wounds
- Operations
- Dental work
- Sick loved ones
- Mental illness
- Stamina
- Diet

We all get anxious and worry about our loved ones when they're not feeling well, and we feel frustrated when we can't help them. Sometimes we are sick ourselves, and we can't get our energy back. If we are not healthy, then it is difficult to be truly happy. Our lives can seem tedious and dreary, and often we end up depressed. Althea is the angel of healing and well-being. Ask through prayer, and she will create more harmony in this area. She will bring cures and hopefulness to improve the situation for us all.

ERIN, THE ANGEL OF PEACE

Altar Accessories
Candle: White
Crystal: Chalcedony
Flower: Lily
Herb: Hyacinth
Incense: Lavender

Prayer day: Sunday

A picture of a white dove

Erin will help with

- World peace
- Feeling safe
- Alleviating anxiety
- A good night's sleep

The world is a minefield of upset and unhappiness, and most of the time we just worry and feel helpless, especially now that television and the Internet bring every part of the Earth's problems into our homes. Our ancestors needed to fret about only their villages or towns, but unfortunately we get to see most of the world's disasters, and it can be very depressing, especially to those who are sensitive. My guide once said to me, "Keep your own home happy and your backyard tidy; if each and every one of you did this, the world would be a better place."

An inability to feel peace of mind and to feel comfortable in our own skin can be very draining. Lying awake at night with our minds churning over events that we cannot control can be soul destroying. Sleep is interrupted and nightmares ensue, leaving us tired and weary in our hearts before we even set out on yet another day of worry. Angelic help is at hand, and we can take the opportunity to grow calm and peaceful again with Erin. If we are given a problem, there will always be a solution somewhere.

GWENDOLYN, THE ANGEL OF PSYCHIC ABILITY

Altar Accessories

Candle: Turquoise, purple, or white

Crystal: Lapis lazuli, moonstone, opal, or tiger's eye

Flower: Orchid

Herb: Star anise or thyme

Incense: Opium

Prayer day: Saturday

Gwendolyn will help with

- Psychic dreams
- Psychic development
- Communicating with loved ones in spirit
- Reading people's minds
- Finding the truth in hidden situations

To grow psychically is the most wonderful thing to experience. Can you imagine looking at someone and sensing whether he or she is good or bad, or best of all, being able to take a peek into the future? What you cannot achieve in the daytime, you can achieve when your mind is in a different consciousness, that is, during dream sleep. Gwendolyn is one of the angels of dream work, and while you sleep, she will come to you and tell you what you need to know. Sleeping with a lapis lazuli or angel's hair crystal on the throat chakra can make our dreams incredibly revealing—with Gwendolyn's help.

JAGO, THE ANGEL OF LAUGHTER AND FUN

Altar Accessories

Candle: Pale green

Crystal: Aventurine

Flower: Buttercup

Herb: Saffron

Incense: Geranium

Prayer day: Saturday

Picture of a clown

Jago will help with

- Bringing optimism
- Laughter and fun
- Parties
- Cheering up the sad
- Making others happy

Jago is the angel of fun and humor. Sometimes we need a good sense of humor to allow us to get through life's daily grind. Laughter is healing, and it brings friendship and optimism. It is far better to be happy than sad, so if your spirits are down and you see no joy in life, invoke the angel Jago to help uplift your hearts and see a more positive side to life. He works well when miserable or negative people who dampen your mood surround you. Ask him to cheer them up as well!

BENEDICT, THE ANGEL OF MEDITATION

Altar Accessories

Candle: Lavender or white

Crystal: Moonstone or opal

Flower: Pansy

Herb: Lemongrass

Incense: Patchouli

Prayer day: Thursday

Benedict will help with

- Getting back to sleep
- Calming your mind
- Clearer focus
- Connecting with your guides and angels
- Tranquility

Benedict, "blessed by God," is the angel who aids meditation and mental focus. Fifteen minutes of meditation can be worth three hours of sleep, so it is essential to master this practice. It is not easy to meditate, because one's mind is apt to wander and to dwell on the trivialities and worries of our busy days. Noise pollution distracts us too. So how do we shut off and find some peace?

Have a personal CD player with earphones, go to bed early, and play meditation music; then invoke Benedict. He is gentle, and he will help you to achieve tranquility. Once you have begun to meditate, you can link with your guides and angels with more freedom. Consider that these wonderful beings are on the end of a telephone line, but you have to find their telephone number. With practice it can be done, especially with Benedict's help.

ZOE, THE ANGEL OF PREGNANCY AND FERTILITY

Altar Accessories

Candle: Blue or pink

Crystal: Coral, rainbow moonstone, or topaz

Flower: Daisy or moss

Herb: Ivy

Incense: Nasturtium

Prayer day: Wednesday

Picture of a baby

Blue or pink ribbons

Zoe will help with

- Fertility
- Safe delivery
- Healthy babies
- Kind doctors and midwives
- Protection against postpartum depression

Zoe is the angel of pregnancy and fertility. If you or a loved one is longing for a child, then ask Zoe to help the pregnancy to come to fruition. Zoe will also protect a woman who is carrying a child and guide her to a safe and happy delivery. If you are anxious about an expectant friend or a female in the family, Zoe will listen to any requests for the safety of the birth for both mother and child.

If you are pregnant, ask Zoe to show you the baby's correct name during dream sleep. Have you ever met someone and felt that his or her name was wrong? Obviously the parents did not heed the wisdom of Zoe before naming their off-spring. The angel Paige can also be used for help with all things pertaining to pregnancy.

GALEN, THE ANGEL OF KNOWLEDGE

Altar Accessories
Candle: Blue
Crystal: Lace agate or pyrite
Flower: Chrysanthemum
Herb: Jasmine
Incense: Jasmine
Prayer day: Friday

Galen will help with

* Exams
* Driving tests
* New knowledge
* Teachers and teaching
* Invention
* Memory

We reincarnate to the Earth plane to gain more knowledge. Knowledge comes from truth, wisdom, and vision. Galen is the angel of intelligence, who encourages us to widen our horizons and grow through study. If you feel stuck and your soul is searching for more information, then invoke the angel Galen for assistance. He will help you to pass an exam, earn a degree, or pass the driving test. If you are a teacher who is unsure of your techniques and teaching skills, call on Galen for help.

DEMETRI, THE ANGEL OF THE ENVIRONMENT

Altar Accessories
Candle: Blue
Crystal: Moss agate, pearl, or emerald
Flower: Sunflower
Herb: Rosemary
Incense: Dewberry
Prayer day: Monday

Demetri will help with

- Community projects
- Housing developments
- Parks and gardens
- Water and air pollution
- Flooding and drought
- Crime-ridden areas

Demetri is the angel for the country or state in which you reside. We all want to feel proud of our environment, so if you live in a dismal area that is ruled by unenlightened people who bring rubbish or disharmony, ask Demetri to restore the balance. Ask him to heighten the consciousness of others so they can learn to respect and love beauty. You can request that he change conditions that have been a problem in the past, such as flooding, drought, or infertile soil. Sometimes a problem is deliberately set before us so we will practice the power of prayer to put it right. Use Demetri to achieve this.

LILLIA, THE ANGEL MESSENGER

Altar Accessories
Candle: Dark purple
Crystal: Opal
Flower: Cyanus or iris
Herb: Yarrow
Incense: Poppy
Prayer day: Tuesday

Lillia will help with

- Informing you of world events and disasters
- Prophesies
- Warnings

Select people are sometimes given prior knowledge when a great disaster is about to occur. It might come in a dream or through automatic writing, meditation, or a sketch that seems to have a mysterious hand guiding the artist to draw the picture. Nostradamus was well-known for his prophesies and predictions. Quite a few people had prior knowledge, in dream sleep, of Princess Diana's death, and some knew beforehand of the World Trade Center tragedy.

My elderly gardener came to see me a week before the September 11 disaster. He showed me a small piece of paper on which he had sketched an image that his guide had given him in dream sleep. At the time it made no sense to me. The drawing contained two tall columns with fire spewing out of the tops of the buildings.

Everything is known in the spirit world. There are no accidents whatsoever, so all is planned. When we have increased our spiritual vibration through meditation and angel counseling, we will be given these wonderful privileges. Lillia will guide us toward gaining precognition.

JAREK, THE ANGEL OF PATIENCE

Altar Accessories
Candle: Yellow
Crystal: Aquamarine
Flower: Alyssum
Herb: Moonflower

Incense: Lavender
Prayer day: Friday

Jarek will help with

- Finishing a project or task
- Patience with others
- Demanding people
- Irritating people
- Stuck-in-the-waiting-room syndrome

How many times have we been impatient with others or ourselves? Perhaps a sick or time-consuming relative or a child is testing your patience and stealing hours from your life. Or a work colleague might be slower than you, making you want to explode with frustration at any moment. You need to remember that your family, friends, and work mates are all part of your life for a reason, and if you have a flaw in your makeup, these people will expose it and inadvertently help you to correct it. We all find ourselves in situations that take us to the edge.

For fifteen years a couple of my old and senile cats were unclean and my patience was tested to the limit, but I feel that Jarek helped me to gain some control over this situation. We must be patient with others, and this can be achieved by invoking the angel Jarek.

ZENIA, THE ANGEL OF FRIENDSHIP

Altar Accessories
Candle: White
Crystal: Bloodstone
Flower: Yellow rose
Herb: Ivy
Incense: Lemon
Prayer day: Thursday

Zenia will help with

- Forming new friendships
- Resolving an argument
- Helping friends
- Reconnecting with old friends

We all know how wonderful it is to have good friends, and some would say they are even better than family. As the old saying goes, "You can choose your friends but not your family." In your lifetime, you will know only a handful of the dearest people; some of them will come along when you are young, and others will become part of your life later on. You will click with some people, and even recognize them as soul mates. Making and keeping friends, though, is an art. You must never ignore your dear friends, and you should always give them your time if they are in situations of distress or illness.

If you are lonely and have few friends, or if you cannot seem to keep the friends you make, Zenia will help to rectify this.

If you need new friends, she will bring the introductions into play. You might want to remain on friendly terms with an ex-partner in order to calm the situation down and start the healing process. This is when Zenia's services are invaluable. Maybe you want someone else to find friends, such as a child or a member of the family. Perhaps you have a wonderful friend in the spirit world that is missed. Zenia will pass on any messages of love you want to give that friend. One of the most distressing situations to occur is when arguments have separated friends. Zenia can repair rifts and help to patch things up. Make a request to Zenia and she will help with all things pertaining to friendship.

PIA, THE ANGEL OF HOPE AND FAITH

Altar Accessories
Candle: Lavender or purple
Crystal: Hematite
Flower: Marigold
Herb: Dill
Incense: Marigold
Prayer day: Tuesday

Pia will help with

- Restoring your faith in someone
- Finding a spiritual faith
- Finding hope
- Optimism

Pia teaches us not to give in; she will find a solution to our problems. Keeping one's faith in life is important, and helping others to keep theirs is imperative. If your life seems hopeless and without happiness, the angel Pia will bring the strength required to look ahead. Faith does not necessarily require a belief in a deity or in religion, but rather the knowledge that something better is ahead when our life is dismal or gray. If a loved one is missing, ask Pia to return that person or to provide information to help find that person. Do not lose hope. Use Pia and remember that your life can change in a day when you believe in angels!

RAOUL, THE ANGEL OF SOUL MATES

Altar Accessories

Candle: Blue

Crystal: Rose quartz

Flower: Tea rose

Herb: Basil

Incense: Rose

Prayer day: Wednesday

Red heart

Raoul will help with

- Connecting with a beloved
- Meeting a beloved in dream sleep
- Getting over the loss of a beloved
- Finding a beloved

It is said that each one of us has our own special soul mate that the Source has created for us. Imagine a circle cut down the middle in which one half is female the other half male. Eventually we return to join our "better half." If we are lucky we might be with our romantic soul mate in this lifetime, but that doesn't always happen, and many people spend their lives looking for this magical person to appear. I have often thought promiscuous types are actually searching for their beloved. When true soul mates unite, if one dies, the other usually departs shortly afterward.

You will have many lives—a few with your beloved, but more without; if you were always with your soul mate, you would be too preoccupied with your soul mate and would not attempt to learn from new relationships. United soul mates have been known to ignore their families, friends, and even their children in pursuit of their obsessive love for each other.

You also have family soul mates, which is why you may be fonder or closer to one child than to the others. A sister or a brother could be a favorite, while you could actively dislike another sibling. We come from a karmic group, and in each life the roles can change. A son might become a brother, a sister a friend, or a mother a daughter in the next life.

The primary soul mate, or beloved, is the most important in your life, and rarely does this role change. If you and your soul mate are both on the planet at the same time and cannot have each other, it can be a very torturous life, filled with unrequited love, yearning, and obsession. Have you known of a situation where someone cannot get over a love affair or the breakup of a marriage? The person carries that love to his or her death and beyond. Unrequited soul mates have been known to commit suicide if they cannot be together; a prime example was Shakespeare's Romeo and Juliet.

Raoul is the angel who will help you in soul mate matters. We might wish to meet our soul mate, or if the soul mate is not on the planet, we can request to be together on the astral plane in dream sleep. Sometimes the beloved will come when we are dreaming, and we may feel that we have been cuddled or kissed and often comforted. A passionate soul mate will even enact sex in dream sleep.

SOFIA, THE ANGEL OF MUSIC AND THE ARTS

Altar Accessories
Candle: Turquoise
Crystal: Topaz
Flower: Angelica
Herb: Coriander
Incense: Citrus
Prayer day: Tuesday
Crayons or paints

Sofia will help with

- Inspiration in the arts
- Writing
- Music composition
- Grace in dance
- Confidence in performance

The beautiful angel Sofia will inspire and enhance your creative abilities or help a member of your family to do so. Children who are studying, singing, dancing, or mastering musical instruments can be helped by her intervention. She can bring concentration and dexterity to little fingers and feet and young voices. Many people find her particularly helpful if exams are pending in the arts or drama. She will give confidence to the nerves of entertainers, ensuring that they give the best performance on the big day.

Ask Sofia to bless creative skills for art. If you paint, but you are stuck for new ideas, she will inspire you with color and creativity. The same applies for sculpting, needlecraft, and baking; interior design and decorating will be helped too. In the spirit world, there are many angels who perform wonderful feats of art, generating beauty that we cannot comprehend or behold. We can be unique in our efforts and inspired with the help and guidance of the angel Sofia.

DOMINIC, THE ANGEL OF MOURNING

Altar Accessories
Candle: Deep purple
Crystal: Obsidian
Flower: Aloe
Herb: Calendula
Incense: Myrrh
Prayer day: Sunday

Dominic will help with

• Healing in the grieving process
• Giving strength when attending funerals
• Rejuvenating the departed soul

Dominic is a very special angel who is responsible for the souls of the departed. As the time for a person's death approaches, he will be nearby to lead the individual to the next stage. He will make sure that person's guide will be present to take him or her back into the spirit world, where other angels of healing will rejuvenate the aura and restore the person to perfect health. Once this has been done, there will be great joy, as the deceased family of the newly passed-over person will be there to welcome him or her back into the family and karmic group.

Dominic's other role is to give strength to the grieving families at the graveside in the months that follow. If there are mass deaths, such as in wars, earthquakes, and other disasters, many angels will attend the departing souls and ensure that they reach the right destination. Angels attend to every soul with minute detail and precision, and there are no mistakes. The day we are born and the day we die are recorded in the Akashic Records in the spiritual world. There is great order, and no stone is left unturned. Dominic can reassure us at all levels of the death process and help us reach the wonderful new life ahead.

GILLAINE, THE ANGEL OF CRUELTY AND REVENGE

Altar Accessories

Candle: Pink

Crystal: Fluorite

Flower: Lily

Herb: Bergamot

Incense: Lavender

Prayer day: Any

A picture of a dove (for peace)

Gillaine will help with

- Abating cruelty
- Containing anger
- Bringing self-control
- Controlling revenge

The angel Gillaine has a special role for those who lash out at others. Some seek to wreak revenge for deeds that have been done to them. Irrational behavior and brutality have followed us through every age of humankind, and the strong have always persecuted the weak. Sometimes mental cruelty can be just as bad as physical cruelty and can affect us throughout our lives. Cruelty comes when an angry victim perpetrates his own misplaced deeds on younger children or defenseless animals, and so the circle continues in its negativity. Gillaine is the angel to approach for these problems. With his help, many situations can be abated and changed forever. For every problem there is a special angel to deal with it.

12

ANGELIC HERBS
AND PLANTS

ANGELICA, THE HERB OF THE ANGELS

Angelica is known as the root of the Holy Spirit; it is also known as wild celery and masterwort.

The angelica plant is linked with the angelic realms, so many people use it for healing, health, and nutrition. Angelica originated in Europe and Asia, and is a member of the parsley family. There are more than fifty varieties; one that has caused a great deal of interest in the United States is angelica sinensis, which is grown in Asia. Its properties are said to regenerate the blood cells and regulate the body rhythms. The plant is sweetly aromatic. It grows as high as eight feet tall.

If you really want to feel connected to the angel vibration, this bright green plant will add a dramatic look to any garden, but it will need moist soil and a partly shady environment. The small oval seeds can be scattered and left for the angels to watch over, or you can cultivate them in a greenhouse. It will most certainly create a fantastic backdrop to any other plants that you have in the garden. One has to bear in mind that it is a biennial and that it will bloom only every two or maybe three years. The roots and seeds have been used for generations to flavor liqueurs such as gin, Benedictine, and absinthe. You can also grind the cooked or dried roots into a powder and add it to cakes, biscuits, and bread. But the most familiar use of this magical plant is in the stems of the angelica, which are colored and sweetened to use in cakes and cake decoration.

Medicinal Uses

- Respiratory ailments
- Allergies
- Anti-inflammatory
- Fever
- Digestive problems
- Premenstrual upsets and hot flashes
- Flatulence
- Stomach cramps
- Promotes the regeneration of red blood cells

Angelica Aromatherapy

A lovely way to relax is to sink into angelica-scented bath water. Just add a few drops of the essential oil to your tub and meditate to connect with your angel. Another way to relax and dispel fatigue and anxiety is to consult an aromatherapist and ask for a massage treatment using a blend of angelica and lavender oils.

CAUTION!

Angelica roots are highly poisonous when fresh, but once dried or cooked they are deemed safe. Expectant mothers, diabetics, and those suffering from heart ailments must not ingest angelica. If you wish to find and pick wild angelica, use extreme caution, as water hemlock looks almost identical and is extremely toxic. If you ingest any plant by mistake, you must seek medical attention immediately!

The Fable of Angelica

We cannot be certain of the origins of this story, but the tale has come down to us through the generations. The story says that in the seventeenth century, a monk communicated with an angel in dream sleep. The angel showed him a magical plant that looked like celery and said the plant would cure the bubonic plague. The angel said it would also heal other ailments, but it would have to be treated with great respect. The wise monk acted upon the angelic information and boiled the roots with treacle and nutmeg spice, blending them into a brew of tea. He then named the plant angelica after the angel. This is where the story gets a bit vague, because no one seems to know the final outcome. We assume that it helped and that the angel's information ensured that the particular form of plague prevalent at the time did die out.

Note:
The bubonic or pneumonic plague has not died out.
It occasionally breaks out in Southeast Asia. Fortunately,
a cocktail of antibiotics cures it very quickly.

THE ANGELIC GARDEN

Some who are devoted to the angelic realms create a garden just for them, even decorating it with statues of angels. If you enjoy gardening, you might want to do the same. Every flower could have the name "angel" in its title. I have listed a few to get you started. But first I must mention one favorite plant of the angels.

Mint

Apparently the angels love the smell of this pungent herb and it is supposed to attract their frequency to the areas where it is grown. There are quite a few varieties of mint, and angels appreciate all of them.

Roses

If you are thinking of planting an angelic rose garden, you might consider some of these striking blooms:

- Golden Angel
- Silver Angel
- Snow Angel
- Los Angeles Frost
- Beautiful Angel

Plants

Plants suitable for an all-angelic garden include:

- Angel's breath (yarrow)
- Angel's trumpet (datura)
- Angel's wing (begonia)
- Blue angel (hosta)
- Guardian angel (hosta)

Trees

If you'd like to include a tree or two to anchor your angel garden, consider these varieties:

- Angel's tree (telegraph plant)
- Angel (horseradish tree)
- Angelica

Iris

Other flowering plants that could be considered for inclusion in your angelic garden are several varieties of iris:

- Angel Chiffon
- Angel Echo
- Angel Heart
- Angel Symphony

If you are really serious about an angel garden, you might want to research the many other plants with "angel" in their names. A good friend of mine who is passionate about gardening told me there are more than 250 species. Happy hunting!

13

ANGELIC CONNECTIONS

In the past, the gods and goddesses have been connected to paganism and witchcraft, and many traditional witches still prefer this form of worship, but there is a modern take on the old ways that we call Angelic Wicca. This is a gentle and spiritual faith that is used for healing and other good causes. One might choose to be a solitary witch or to join a coven with like-minded individuals. Modern-day white witches invoke angels when spell casting, using different angels for different situations.

THE ANGELIC COVEN

A coven is a form of church or spiritual gathering, and just as Christians pray to the angels, so do Wiccan witches. There is much stigma attached to covens and witches. They are supposedly in league with the devil and his entourage of demons and fiends. Images of naked, warty crones whizzing through the air on gnarled besoms at midnight paint a macabre picture, not to mention a coven of witches chanting and dancing naked around the flames of a huge bonfire!

Books, film, and television, like *Bewitched, Charmed,* and the Harry Potter series, have done much to take away the sinister side of witchcraft. Children have always been at ease with magic; they take it in stride. When asked what he wanted for Christmas, my eldest grandson requested . . . a wand!

Coven witches will send prayers to specific angels at certain phases of the moon, because, when they work as a group, their powers are amplified to achieve a better result. If one coven member has a sick relative, a message will be sent out to the other witches for help. The group will act as a family of like-minded soul sisters or soul brothers, working together to solve a variety of problems, and the bonds formed within such a coven are strong and enduring. Many Wiccans believe they cannot choose their blood family; angelic witches believe their coven is their family.

ANGELS AND COINCIDENCE

Angels seem to favor the synchronicity of three. If asking for a favor from them in meditation or prayer, it can be helpful to repeat it three times to give the request more weight. Angels will often make things happen in threes to let us know we are on the right track in our lives. They are

extremely playful and fun loving, so they will create small miracles that we see as coincidences.

When I began writing this book and had just started to write a certain word, at that exact moment on the radio the announcer said the same word. This has happened so many times since then that I have lost count. I am sure it is not coincidental. At other times a pop song with the word "angel" in the title would be sung on the radio when I was typing. As I said earlier, angelic messages are very subtle, and there is always that question mark: Did I imagine that? Did they really do that for me? They did!

ANGELS AND HYPNOTHERAPY

Some of us find it very hard to meditate and connect with an angel or a guide. We might be easily distracted or the mind will wander off to more mundane things. In this case, hypnotherapy can be helpful, especially if we find a hypnotherapist who is sensitive and sympathetic to angelic work. My husband is a clinical hypnotherapist and has taken me on many journeys where I have been able to connect with my angel and guides. One might say, "Why do this when you can meditate instead?" I tried it purely as an experiment, and I found it very helpful.

Some of my husband's clients have asked specifically to be hypnotized to the point of their death in their previous life and then beyond that. Then they have met their guides and angels who have taken them back to greet their families and their karmic group. My daughter did this and was amazed at how many of her karmic group she had forgotten! To be fair, she was a little unsettled for a few days after the session, because she felt a strong sense of sadness and she yearned to be back with them. If you do decide to try this, remember that it is not for the fainthearted, so be sure that your character is strong enough to take it. It can be hard to live in two worlds!

Some wannabe hypnotherapists take a weekend course and then profess to be highly qualified. The person you use should have studied at least two to three years before you can feel confident with them, so check their credentials to be on the safe side.

DYNAMIC ANGEL HEALING

When a person is very depressed and holds a sadness within that he or she cannot seem to remove, an angel will often intervene to restore the balance. I have heard many stories of this sort of vibrational healing, and I have experienced it once or twice myself. The healing will usually happen in the early hours of the morning when one is asleep. It is quite hard to explain this phenomenon, but I will try my best.

One feels in a trancelike state; then suddenly an energy field of pure white light is forced into the solar plexus; then one feels as though one is being lifted off the bed. An electrical energy or a buzzing current runs up and down the body for a minute or so. Sometimes the noise of electrical crackling is heard. At this stage the person is probably semiconscious and could open his or her eyes, but it is best to go with the sensation, eyes closed, and not be afraid. Afterward, feelings of floating or suspension will prevail for about five minutes or so . . . and then sleep comes again. When one wakes up the next morning, all sadness will have disappeared and the body will be refreshed and energized.

THE CHURCH
OF ST. RAPHAEL

Recently my husband and I decided to take a drive on Dartmoor, which is a plateau in the southern part of England, in a county called Devon.

It was a beautiful February day, slightly overcast but with rays of sunshine casting little rainbows in the sky. As we meandered along, we admired the swollen gray rivers and fast-running streams crashing against the granite. The wild ponies and sheep were intent on grazing the short-cropped grasses on the moorland hills, and they appeared content and fat. Casually I remarked to my husband we were in the area of a church that a friend had told me about. It was called St. Raphael's and it had been built in 1869. Without much difficulty, we managed to locate the little chapel, which overlooked a winding silver river. Around the building were thousands of pure white snowdrops forming a pathway to the church and its perimeter. Outside, propped against the gate, was a handwritten notice that said, "Please come in and view our snowdrops." My husband said, "Well, shall we go in?" I sighed. "It will be locked. Churches today are always locked." Not to be thwarted, he opened the latched double wooden gates and grabbed my hand. "Come on; let's at least take a look." He pushed the arched blue door open and we stepped tentatively inside the tiny church. There was a hushed stillness as we looked around, and strangely, I felt that the chapel was inspecting us. Sitting down on one of the ancient wooden pews, I looked above the simple altar at a stained-glass window of the angel Raphael, resplendent in colors of magenta, amber, and indigo. For a few months, I had not been well and had spent time in doctors' offices and hospitals. I closed my eyes and for some reason felt a sad lump come into my throat. I wondered if Raphael would heal me, as I had come to his very special place. Silently, I composed a small prayer and asked him to cleanse me of any illness.

We left the church and strolled around the grounds, feasting our eyes on the carpet of snowdrops. On the journey home, we were both lost in our own thoughts; then my husband turned to me and said quietly, "You know you've been given healing in the church today, don't you?" I nodded as I watched the grassy banks whiz by in a green blur and was amazed that he had linked into the situation. A few days later I felt better than I had for a couple of years, and I thanked Raphael for his loving care in the simple little church on Dartmoor.

In theory, we don't need to go to a church or any other sanctified place to receive healing, because angels can give us healing anywhere, but small out-of-the-way churches are usually quiet and peaceful. Here we can get away from the noise and rush of daily life for an hour or so, relax our jangled nerves, and allow our hearts and minds to open up and let the angels come to our aid.

ANGELS OF DISASTERS

The angels of disasters have prior knowledge of all the catastrophes on Earth, and no one is overlooked when help is needed. Each and every one of us will be watched with close attention and devotional love. Some of us will have to die courageously, while others will live to see another day. There are no mistakes in the divine plan as to who goes and who stays.

Often these terrible events occur to make human beings value life and to make us form a stronger community spirit. After all, we are all brothers and sisters. Out of grief and sadness come wisdom and maturity. In the last two world wars, the community spirit was notable, as others looked out for each family in their town or village. Today's society has lost this vital ingredient. Now we are squirreled away in our own homes staring at computers or television screens. Our offspring are lost in their own worlds, with imaginary people in computer games and DVDs, and some have little knowledge of family values. I must hold my own hand up and say that I know very little of some of my neighbors, not even their names! Sixty years ago, this would have been unthinkable!

When tragedy strikes, everything becomes real and we all start to pull together. Disasters can show the courage or the cowardice within our souls. A timid person might suddenly save another's life, while a so-called hero will turn and run to save his or her own skin. Any person who has come face-to-face with death will always say that the experience has made him or her a better and more knowledgeable person. If we decide to give our lives to save another in a horrific moment, the rewards on returning to the spirit world are incredible.

Angels take pride in our feats, especially if we have valued someone else's life above our own. These beings watch every person closely and note well those who need to be tested in a dangerous situation.

ALCOHOL, DRUGS, AND ANGELS

Alcohol relieves stress and is used by most of the inhabitants of the world when they want to unwind. I enjoy a nice glass of red wine, and alcohol can brighten up many a social occasion. Unfortunately, if we drink too much, it can stop our guides and angels from getting in touch with us, especially during dream sleep. Heavy drinking in the evening makes a person more or less pass out when going to bed and will often leave one open to psychic attack because the individual is literally "out of it." Bad dreams or nightmares ensue, and interrupted sleep spoils the natural rhythm of the body. Care must be taken with alcohol, as consuming too much is frowned upon by the angelic realms.

Much the same goes for prescription or over-the-counter drugs. A couple of Aspirin probably won't hinder a connection with the angelic realm, but such things as Prozac, other tranquilizers, sleeping pills, and so on are designed to put up a barrier between us and a world with which we find too painful to cope. If, as it seems, angels need a "clean environment" to work with, these drugs must also act as a barrier to contact.

Perhaps overdosing on food has the same effect. After all, comfort eating is designed to distance us from pain, so it would surely detach us from the spiritual realms as well.

A brother of the White Eagle Lodge once told me that our angels like "clean vessels" to work with, and drinking will inevitably block any connections with them. This also applies to people who take drugs to escape the life-learning processes that the Creator has put in place for them. We are never given anything we cannot handle, so blurring the mind with alcohol or doping ourselves into oblivion is just the equivalent of sticking our heads in the sand, and it will stop our karmic development. If we skip our lessons in this life, our next one will still have the same problems or obstacles to deal with, but perhaps with no drugs or alcohol in sight! So in effect, there is no way out; we have just got to get on with it and face our trials and tribulations!

14

ANGELS IN
THE AFTERLIFE

I talked a little about the spirit world in earlier chapters, but I will return to the subject now. Many people who have had a near-death experience talk of a beautiful white tunnel that pulls them upward and strong feelings of peace and excitement on returning to the spirit world. An angel or a guide will be present with us until we are safely there. Family members who have previously died will often meet the returning soul, and the joy is indescribable. When children die, a beloved pet will often be there to greet and comfort them. After the reunions, we are taken to a special place where the healing angels go into action to reenergize the aura and cleanse any sadness and pain from the returning soul. There are special temples and rooms of exquisite light and rarefied atmospheres where this healing process is undertaken. A long deep sleep will refresh the person, who will awaken later with no ill effects from the previous life and with renewed zest for the new life ahead.

THE ANGELS OF JUDGMENT

The next process is the judgment. This is not to be feared, as the angels of judgment are very gentle and understanding. They will never reprimand or chastise us for any wrong done in our previous life. Their frequency is unconditional love. Regardless of our deeds, as negative as they might have been, we will not faze the angels of judgment. Their job is to take us to a special place where we will be shown a sort of video of our life. The viewing starts with childhood and follows through to the last moments. All we have obtained is shown, and any negative actions are shown, without censorship. We then judge ourselves for each second of our life on Earth. We see what we achieved and note the opportunities we might have lost, and we see how our behavior has affected others. No stone is left unturned, so the experience is quite moving and powerful.

If we are truly remorseful for any harm done, we are immediately forgiven and the slate is wiped clean on that issue. If we are unrepentant, then we will have to face the troublesome issue in another lifetime. After the judgment, the angels will ask why we handled a situation in a certain way and how we could have avoided it. Often, returning souls are shocked to discover that a thought is a living thing! We should never think of harming anyone; even though the deed might not actually have been done, that thought is still out there.

ANGELS OF APPAREL

Once the soul is judged, the angels of apparel show how we will appear to others. There are no secrets in the spirit world, and we cannot hide our faults from anyone. Each soul has a vibration of light and color that surrounds it. This "garment" is a robe that represents the subject's true character and levels of failure and achievements. Within the colors, there are shades that depict each person's character, so, for instance, if we were kind to animals, that would be shown by one specific shade, while a bully would exhibit a different color. Collectively, the garment or robe could be stunningly beautiful or utterly disappointing. Our karmic groups are usually on the same wavelengths and have the same shades, faults, and attributes as ourselves.

As we progress through the system, the story shown in the robe will improve. Sometimes a beloved soul mate that has moved on will stay and help the struggling person to step up the ladder and improve the colors or his or her garment. The angels of apparel are always present to encourage and inspire the souls to better themselves.

Note:
The colors of angels' robes are magnificent and beautiful. There are no blemishes or ugliness; just perfection, light, and wonderment.

ANGELS OF REINCARNATION

After the soul has been in the spirit world for a while, it will be able to choose whether it returns to Earth to gain more wisdom and perhaps to redress the wrongs that have been perpetrated in previous lives. Caring angels and guides will discuss what sort of life would be best, including the type of parents and siblings, the person's race, religion, and cultural group, and the country the individual is to be born into. The "committee" even discusses the kind of body the reincarnating soul will have. Many lives can be with the same group or family, but roles can be reversed. A mother can become a sister, while a grandson could become a son, and so on. If an individual had a serious issue with another person in a previous life, that individual will be asked to give it another try, until the balance can be restored.

We do not have to reincarnate, but it helps us to move along quickly and to gain a deeper empathy for life and its problems. It would be sad to be left behind without our karmic group, especially if the other members are succeeding in their own special development and moving away from us.

NICKI

Nicki has been a friend of mine for many years. She has dedicated herself to nursing and specializes in working with children. Others in her family have been connected with medicine, and her own husband is a very well-loved and respected doctor.

About fifteen years ago, Nicki was in a phase where she felt as if she had hit rock bottom, and she could not lose the depression that had descended upon her. One early spring morning, she decided to take a walk in a wood not far from where she lived. It was a quiet place that she had always loved, especially as there was a small, lively river running alongside it. As she walked along, she stared down disconsolately at her feet, trying hard not to give in to the depression that was gripping her. From out of nowhere, an invisible hand placed itself firmly on her chest, stopping her dead in her tracks. Suddenly four angels in iridescent white robes with golden wings encircled her; she was amazed at how tall they were, and she was struck by their androgynous beauty and long golden hair. Gently, their wings enfolded Nicki and lifted her higher and higher into a place of total love and peace. They told her that this was the one and only true reality and that she must not forget that, as all else was just an illusion.

Then they instructed her to look down into the wood. She saw herself as a little speck in her short blue coat among the bare trees, and the little person that she saw appeared to be sad and helpless. The angels gave her healing and unconditional love, and lifted her spirits. Then, with her eyes tightly closed, she felt her feet connect with the ground on the woodland path. She longed to return to the angels and the place of tranquility that she had been so privileged to visit, but knew she had to stay and continue to be of service to others in her job. After this connection with the angels, Nicki was totally revived and happy, and now if she goes through a bad patch, she remembers her encounter with the four wonderful angels and gains strength and fortitude.

conclusion

If we take some time to dedicate ourselves to others in this lifetime, we become very precious to the angelic beings when we return to the spirit world. Teachers, veterinarians, nurses, doctors, health-care workers, life coaches, and individuals who perform any other job that improves the lives of others are valued by the angels. They give us rewards beyond imagination when we return to our true home, which is the spiritual world. We become closer to the Source or Creator.

We are only visitors to this planet, and this is our schoolroom. What we sow is what we eventually reap.

May the angels in Heaven bless you and keep you safe for the rest of your journey on Earth.

acknowledgments

Thanks to Leanna Greenaway and John Greenaway, who helped and supported me while I wrote this book. I would like to acknowledge Louise Cheval, who provided information on some of the crystals used in the prayers. A special thank you to Nicki Bellamy, a private person who shared the story of her encounter with the angels. Also, thanks to Adele and Mark Lewis and Justin Lewis for their contributions. Thanks to Dr. Rosalind Cooling, who has inspired me to believe there really are "Earth angels" on the planet, and lastly my thanks go to Sasha Fenton, a prolific author and publisher who gave me the opportunity to write this book.

index